for the love of LICORICE

60 LICORICE-INSPIRED CANDIES, DESSERTS, MEALS, AND MORE

ELISABETH JOHANSSON
PHOTOGRAPHY BY HELÉN PE

Skyhorse Publishing

Skyhorse Publishing books may be purchased in bulk at special discounts for sales promo-
tion, corporate gifts, fund-raising, or educational purposes. Special editions can also be
created to specifications. For details, contact the Special Sales Department, Skyhorse Publishing, 307 West 36th Street, 11th Floor, New York, NY 10018 or info@skyhorsepublishing.com.

Skyhorse® and Skyhorse Publishing® are registered trademarks of
Skyhorse Publishing, Inc.®, a Delaware corporation.

Visit our website at www.skyhorsepublishing.com.

10 9 8 7 6 5 4 3 2 1

Library of Congress Cataloging-in-Publication Data is available on file.

Cover design by Eva-Jo Hancock
Cover photo credit Helén Pe

Print ISBN: 978-1-5107-1293-5
Ebook ISBN: 978-1-5107-1297-3

Printed in China

Raw licorice stick

Licorice roots

Ground licorice root

Licorice Granules

Raw licorice pastilles

CONTENTS

LICORICE FACTS: INTERESTING READING ABOUT THE BEST AND TASTIEST ROOT IN THE WORLD

RECIPES: LICORICE IN EVERYTHING FROM PRALINES, ICE CREAM, AND PASTRIES TO CHOCOLATE MOUSSE, FISH SOUP, AND SCHNAPPS

TASTE, EXPERIMENT, MORE FACTS: TIPS AND ADVICE

I HAVE WORKED WITH LICORICE IN DIFFERENT FORMS FOR MANY YEARS, AND I LOOK FORWARD TO SHARING THOSE EXPERIENCES AND RECIPES WITH YOU.

My great interest in licorice began when I first had the opportunity to try licorice as a seasoning. I was never a big fan of licorice candy, but when I discovered the possibilities licorice had as a seasoning, it was a real "aha moment" for me. The first combination I tried was licorice and chocolate, quite unusual at the time, but I found it to be a fantastic combination!

I immediately started experimenting with licorice—baking, making desserts and ice cream—and discovered there were many great "flavor friends" that it went well with. Later, I even began flavoring some hot dishes with licorice. It was so much fun discovering how incredibly versatile licorice is.

Over the years I've found many others who have learned how good licorice is with food and sweets, and a growing number of people are curious about it. I notice it most of all when I give lectures and hold licorice tastings.

In this book I share my licorice favorites, everything from cookie, cake, ice cream, and hot dish recipes to a healthy, throat soothing tea. And, maybe best of all, you'll learn how to make real licorice candy, such as English confectionery and hard licorice caramels!

I will also take you on a journey to Calabria, Italy, where a lot of licorice is grown (it can also be found in the wild). Visiting a licorice factory, I got to witness with my own eyes how they refine the licorice roots into raw licorice. More about this fantastic voyage begins on page 12.

Enjoy licorice!
Elisabeth Johansson

LICORICE (*GLYCYRRHIZA*)

The licorice root's Greek name, *Glycyrhiza* is a combination of the words *glycy*, sweet, and *rhiza*, which are all roots. In English, licorice, licorice root, sweet wood, and sweet licorice are common terms. The British spelling is liquorice, while in American English it is spelled licorice. In Swedish, it's *lakrits*.

Licorice is made from the root of a bush-like perennial herb that is part of the legume family. It has a branched stem, scalloped leaves, and mauve flowers that grow in bundles where the leafstalk and the stem meet. The fruit itself is a maroon pod.

The licorice plant can grow anywhere along the same latitude, but grows mostly in the Mediterranean region, including Italy, France, and Spain. It can also be found in Russia, China, Iran and other parts of the Middle East, Egypt, and some parts of North America and Australia. Some of the licorice roots used in production today grow in the wild, but commercial licorice is grown in Western Europe.

It is said that the best licorice can be found in Calabria, Italy, where licorice has been cultivated since the eighteenth century. In Calabria, you can enjoy a cup of coffee flavored with licorice and have a scoop of licorice ice cream on the side! Iran is also a major licorice-producing county.

Some Species of Licorice:

Glycyrrhiza glabra is the most common licorice root in Scandinavia and Europe. It grows in Europe, Asia, North America, and Australia.

Glycyrrhiza acanthocarpa grows in Australia.

Glycyrrhiza lepidota grows in North America.

Glycyrrhiza uralensis grows in China and western Asia.

Glycyrrhiza inflata grows in China and Asia.

Glycyrrhiza echinata grows in Russia.

The Twin Flavors of Licorice

There is a distinct taste of licorice in anise and star anise. Although these plants are not related to licorice, they do contain similar substances. In anise and star anise, the substance anethole is what reminds us of the sweetness of licorice. Fresh fennel also tastes a bit like licorice, but that flavor disappears if the fennel is heated.

Herbs like chervil and tarragon also taste of licorice—the latter a bit more. This is said to be caused by the substance estragole. In licorice, the glycosine glycyrrhizin causes the special flavor. Because the taste of the glycyrrhizin lingers, it's difficult to find a complementary beverage to pair with it.

REFINED LICORICE PRODUCTS

Licorice is the raw material. Listed below are the refined products made from it. Use the whole licorice root for cooking if possible. Let it boil in stews or similar dishes, just as you would with bay leaves.

■ **Licorice roots** from different areas also look different. To the left are roots from Iran. To the right are the maroon roots from Italy.

■ **Ground licorice root** is a bright yellow powder made from dried, ground licorice roots without additives. The powder has a mild, natural, sweet licorice flavor and goes well with fish, seafood, pastries, and desserts.

■ **Raw licorice** in sticks, blocks, or diced is hard, one hundred percent raw licorice. It can be grated or crushed and then used for flavoring hot dishes, desserts, and candy.

■ **Liquid licorice** extract may contain food coloring, preservatives, and flavor enhancers, like anise. It's used for confectioneries, ice cream, desserts, and pastries.

■ **Raw licorice pastilles** are mostly consumed as the candy they are, but they can also be crushed and used for flavoring pastries and hot dishes.

■ **Licorice granules** are made by grinding or crushing sticks or blocks of raw licorice. Granules are used for foods, desserts, ice cream, candy, and pastries.

■ **Licorice powder** is made by spray-drying the licorice mass. It becomes a fine brown powder that is easily soluble. It may contain malt sugar and works well in desserts, ice cream, candy, and pastries.

■ **Salty licorice powder** is licorice powder mixed with salmiak salt. Used for desserts, ice cream, candy, and pastries.

A LICORICE VOYAGE TO CALABRIA

In order to experience the origin of licorice and understand the processing of raw licorice from the start, I traveled to the Amarelli licorice factory. The factory is located in the village of Rossano in southern Italy. Amarelli has a long tradition of licorice production and has been making raw licorice for nearly 300 years!

There, in the Calabria region along the coast of the Ionian Sea, licorice grows in the wild. It often grows along the beaches or between fields, but sometimes it even grows between the paving stones!

About forty years ago there were approximately eighty large and medium licorice factories in the region, but today only two large factories remain: Amarelli and Naturmed.

In Italy, licorice is primarily consumed as a candy, but it's also used as a flavoring for grappa, ice cream, and coffee, among other things.

Visiting the Amarelli Licorice Factory
Upon my arrival at the factory, I found heaps and heaps of licorice roots, some up to nine yards long. Amarelli buys the roots from neighboring farmers who grow their own and also harvest wild roots. Pulling up the roots is hard work and must be done with a tractor.

When the licorice roots arrive at the factory, they are washed and dried thoroughly. Then they are sorted by size, and the finer roots are cut into six-inch-long pieces. These pieces are then packed by hand.

Juice is extracted from the remaining roots. To extract the juice, the roots are chopped up and steam-boiled under pressure for three to four hours. The juice is boiled at 320° F until it turns into a viscous mass. The mass is then processed with large blades, which also adds oxygen to the mass. This makes the licorice oxidize and it becomes dark brown-black in color.

Next, the mass is pressed together into blocks or sticks. The sticks are cut into smaller pieces and left to dry with the blocks on big drying racks. Some of the mass is used to make licorice pastilles. Most of it is kept natural, but some is flavored, for example, with mint. When the pastilles are made they have a matte finish, but after going through a steam bath the finish turns nice and glossy.

I also visited Amarelli's licorice museum, where you can learn about the factory's fascinating history. Here you will also find a wonderful collection of documents and magazines about licorice from all over the world.

It was a fantastic journey. To see all the steps that go into processing licorice with my own eyes was more interesting than I had hoped. That something so natural can taste so good and be so useful was really eye—and taste bud—opening!

If you ever plan a visit to Calabria, take the time to visit the licorice museum. You can schedule a visit to the museum at info@museodellaliquirizia.it.

1. Licorice seeds.

2. Newly sprouted licorice seeds.

GROW YOUR OWN LICORICE

The licorice plant (*Glycyrrhiza glabra*) is a vigorous and beautiful perennial plant that would look wonderful in any herb garden. It thrives in both sun and semi-shade and grows to about 4 feet in height, but it can grow even taller in the wild. It sprouts in one to three months, and the plant blooms from July to September.

Licorice seeds sprout slowly and very irregularly. The seeds should be started in a well-drained pot filled with a sand and soil mix or Mediterranean soil. Alternatively, the soil can be mixed with perlite. Plant the seeds at a depth of about ¼ inch. February or March is a good time to plant the seeds. Once the plants have sprouted and the leaves are starting to become visible, it's time to replant them in larger pots. It's also possible to sow directly in the ground or into outdoor pots in May through September, depending on your location. Cover with a thin layer of perlite.

3. Time to change to a bigger pot.

4. The licorice root after two to three years.

The plants should be covered in winter, and since they are sensitive to cold, they can be replanted into pots (big plastic pots or bottomless buckets) and taken into a greenhouse in milder regions.

Harvesting of the roots should be done once the plant is about three to four years old.

LICORICE—THE HEALTHY ROOT

People have used the licorice root as a medicinal plant for centuries. For example, in ancient Greece and the Roman empire it was used against asthma and the common cold. It was even more widely used as a medicinal plant in Ancient China . . . and its use continues there today.

In the Nordic countries, pharmacies started selling it during the sixteenth century as an expectorant and a cure for ailing stomachs. Licorice was still available at pharmacies there as late as the 1970s.

Internal Use

Mouth: Anti-inflammatory and preventing cavities. Some say that chewing the licorice root was the forerunner to modern-day toothbrushing. Now there is toothpaste that is flavored with licorice.

Throat: Expectorant and inflammation-reducing effects. Among other things, licorice contains saponins, a soap-like substance that lowers the surface tension in mucous membranes. The saponins activate the reflexes in the bronchus, making it easier to expel mucous.

Stomach and intestines: Encourages healing and has been used for a long time for upset stomachs and intestines. Licorice contains large quantities of flavonoids, which are believed to suppress the helicobacter pylori bacteria in sore stomachs. Eating regular quantities of licorice may also have a laxative effect.

Kidney and adrenal gland: Believed to have a stimulating effect.

Liver: Believed to have a positive effect on a damaged liver, but also believed to have a protective effect in general.

Genitals: Licorice is said to be helpful in relieving menstrual cramps and in treating urinary tract infections.

External Use

Skin and hair: Licorice has been used in skin products for a long time. In Asia, it is common to find licorice in products for treating acne and psoriasis. Licorice is believed to have a healing effect on exuding wounds, rashes, and eczema. They also make shampoo with licorice, which can have a positive effect on the scalp. In addition, licorice has been used for a long time in the treatment of herpes, both herpes labialis and genital herpes.

Since licorice has a minor bleaching effect on the skin, skin care products with licorice can be used to help lighten irregular pigments and spots. However, they should not be used when tanning.

The licorice root contains around 20 fungus-reducing substances, which might help in treating athlete's foot.

HOUSEHOLD REMEDIES WITH LICORICE

Throat Tea with Licorice, Sage, and Peppermint

A nice, warming tea that is good for the throat. Licorice is an expectorant and can help calm a cough. The peppermint helps to open the airways, and the slightly antibiotic sage soothes the throat and can speed healing.

1 cup water
1 licorice root
3 twigs of fresh peppermint
3 stems of fresh sage
honey, optional
1 small jug

Boil the water and licorice root in a small pan. Remove from the heat and add the peppermint. Let it steep for a few minutes. Add the sage and let it steep several more minutes. Sift, then add some honey if desired.

For coughs: Chew licorice root or drink brewed tea with crushed licorice root. Another option is to combine some ground licorice root with honey and add it to a glass of hot water, then drink the water.

For throat inflammation: Drink tea brewed with crushed licorice root, dried chamomile, and sage.

Moisturizing Licorice Hand Bath

A moisturizing and beautiful hand bath that is healthy for both body and soul.

½ tsp. ground licorice root
2 tsp. flaky sea salt
½–1 tsp. dried lavender
a few drops of peppermint oil
a few drops of ecological soap, prefera-
  bly licorice soap
½ gallon of lukewarm water

Mix licorice root, salt, lavender, and peppermint oil together in a bowl. Next, add some soap, then add some fresh flowers and start adding the water. Let your hands rest in the water for 5 to 10 minutes. Then, rinse your hands and dry them thoroughly. Rub your hands with an oil or hand cream.

RECIPES

CANDY

English Licorice Confectionery

■ Sweets that are fun to make! And isn't it fun to know how to make your own English confections? Ensuring you have the correct measurements for the ingredients is important when making these sweets, so I've stated the weight of the ingredients for this recipe.

MAKES: 20 PIECES

Licorice mass
4 sheets of gelatin
⅙ oz. licorice granules
3 oz. water
⅙ oz. liquid malt or dark corn syrup
2⅓ oz. cane sugar
¾ oz. flour

Filling
3½ oz. marzipan
3 tbsp. grated coconut
½ fl. oz. glucose

Let the gelatin for the licorice mass sit in a bowl of cold water for 5–10 minutes. Combine the licorice granules, water, liquid malt, cane sugar, and flour in a saucepan. While stirring continuously, boil and bring the mixture to 185° F or until it starts to thicken. Remove the saucepan from the heat. Take the gelatin sheets from the water, put them in the warm mixture, and stir until the sheets have melted.

Pour the warm licorice mixture onto a silicone baking mat then use a palette knife to spread it out into a thin rectangle. Let it harden for 1–2 days at room temperature.

Finely grate the marzipan, then mix it with the coconut and glucose. Roll out the marzipan filling between pieces of plastic wrap to about the same size as the licorice rectangle. Then put the marzipan over the licorice, leaving about ¼ inch without filling along the upper edge of the licorice rectangle.

Form it into a roll; you may need to add a little water along the edge to make it stick together. Using a sharp knife, slice the roll into approximately 20 pieces. This confection will last a couple of weeks in an airtight jar.

Licorice Balls

■ Boost your day with energetic licorice balls and a fresh, cold smoothie.

MAKES: 35 PIECES

12 soft, dried, seeded dates
1 cup cashew nuts (about 7 oz.)
3 tbsp. cocoa powder
1 tbsp. coconut oil or butter
1 tsp. licorice granules or salty licorice powder
7 oz. dark chocolate, 56–70%
2 tsp. licorice granules
paper petit fours molds

Let the dates soak in cold water for 10 minutes, then drain. Blend the cashew nuts finely, then add the dates and blend together. Add the cocoa powder, coconut oil, and licorice granules. Blend into a smooth paste, then put the mixture in the refrigerator for 30 minutes.

Once chilled, roll the paste into balls. Finely chop 2 oz. of dark chocolate and melt it carefully in the microwave, ensuring that it does not burn. Finely chop the remaining dark chocolate, then mix it with licorice granules on a flat plate. Put some of the melted chocolate in your palm and roll one of the balls in your hand, covering it with the chocolate. Next, roll the ball in the chocolate and licorice mix. Repeat this procedure with the rest of the balls. Place them into the paper molds and store in an airtight container in the refrigerator. These will last for several weeks.

Peach Smoothie Topped with Raw Licorice and Coconut

■ An ice cold and amazingly tasty smoothie.

SERVINGS: 4

8 oz. peaches or frozen, diced mango
2 bananas, diced
1⅔ cups pineapple juice
1 tsp. licorice granules
2 tbsp. dried coconut chips or grated coconut

Dice and core the peaches, then place them in the freezer for 1 hour (or use frozen, diced mango).

Blend the fruit and juice with a stick blender. Pour into glasses and top with the licorice granules and coconut.

Licorice Butterscotch with Chili

■ Licorice and chili in a butterscotch as smooth as silk!

MAKES: 35 PIECES

1¼ cups cane sugar
3½ fl. oz. glucose
3 oz. butter
1 cup heavy cream
2 tsp. licorice granules or 3 tsp. licorice
    powder
optional: 2 drops of liquid licorice aroma
    or salty licorice aroma
optional: a few drops of black food
    coloring
1–2 tsp. sea salt
1–2 tsp. chili flakes

In a heavy-bottomed saucepan, boil the sugar and glucose together into amber butterscotch. The mix should boil to 340° F. Stir carefully a few times.

Meanwhile, heat the butter, cream, and licorice granules in another saucepan. Take both pans off the stove. Add the cream mixture very slowly and carefully into the butterscotch (note that the butterscotch will sizzle). Put the saucepan back on the stove and boil to 256° F, stirring occasionally. Use caution, as it can possibly boil over and create a mess.

Do a ball test, then add the liquid licorice aroma and/or black food coloring, if desired, and stir.

Pour the paste into a 7 x 6-inch pan lined with parchment paper. Once the butterscotch has hardened a little, sprinkle the sea salt and chili flakes over the top. Let the butterscotch harden overnight at room temperature. Once hardened, cut it into pieces using a knife that has been coated with a neutral cooking oil and dried. Wrap the pieces in plastic or parchment paper. Store the butterscotch in an airtight container at room temperature or in the refrigerator.

Chocolate-Dipped Licorice Butterscotch

Cook a batch of the licorice butterscotch, but do not sprinkle on the sea salt and chili flakes. Chop and temper 7 oz. of milk or dark (56–70%) chocolate, (see page 36 for instructions). Cut the butterscotch as described above, then dip the pieces in the tempered chocolate. Sprinkle sea salt over the pieces then let them harden. (See the picture on page 41.)

Salmiak and Licorice Butterscotch

Cook a batch of the licorice butterscotch, but do not sprinkle on the sea salt and chili flakes. Instead, sprinkle with some salmiak salt once the butterscotch has hardened a little. (See the picture on page 133.)

Ball Test

Drip some butterscotch batter into a glass of cold water. If the butterscotch can be rolled into a ball, it is ready. At 250° F, the ball is rather soft; at 255° F it becomes harder.

French Licorice Toffee

■ I would bet nobody can resist these wonderful sweets with licorice and dark chocolate—not even those who normally don't like licorice.

MAKES: 25–30 PIECES

7 oz. dark chocolate (70%)
1 cup cane sugar
1 tbsp. honey
¾ cup heavy cream
2 tsp. licorice powder
2–3 drops liquid licorice aroma
⅓ oz. butter, room temperature
optional: black food coloring
1–2 tsp. sea salt

Chop the chocolate. Put the sugar and honey in a small saucepan and let it boil to about 340° F. Do not stir or the light brown caramel may crystallize. Just shake the saucepan carefully a few times.

Heat the cream in the microwave until it is lukewarm, then add the licorice powder. Remove the saucepan of caramel from the stove, then slowly and carefully stir in the cream mixture (beware that the caramel will sizzle). Stirring occasionally, boil until the mixture is nice and smooth and has a temperature of 260° F, which should take about 5 minutes. Use caution, the sugar and cream will boil rapidly. Take the saucepan off the heat, then add the chocolate, liquid licorice aroma, and butter. If desired, add the black food coloring as well. Stir.

Pour the mixture into a 4 x 9-inch parchment-lined baking pan. Once the mixture has hardened, sprinkle the sea salt over the top.

Let it sit at room temperature for about 12 hours, or overnight. Cut into pieces using a sharp knife. Store in an airtight container with wax paper between the layers.

Tip!
To make it easier to slice the toffee, coat the knife with neutral cooking oil, dry the knife, then cut the toffee into even-sized pieces.

Licorice Caramels

■ If you have a marble counter, there's no need for a silicone mat to make these caramels. Just oil your counter and start! If you'd like a flavor that reminds you of classic cough drops, add a few drops of peppermint and anise oil to the caramel mass.

MAKES: 150 PIECES

2–3 tbsp. sunflower or rapeseed oil
¼ cup + 2 tbsp. water
2⅓ cups cane sugar (16 oz.)
¾ cup + 1½ tbsp. dextrose (4½ oz.)
6–8 drops liquid licorice aroma
black food coloring
several drops of neutral oil for the scissors

For this recipe you will need one or two dough scrapers, a pair of scissors, and a pair of rubber gloves.

Place a kitchen towel on a table or countertop, place a sheet pan over the towel, then place a silicone mat on the pan. Brush the oil onto the silicone mat. (If your silicone mat is thin, you can tape it to the edges of the pan to stop it from moving.)

Stir together the water, cane sugar, and dextrose in a stainless steel saucepan. Boil the mixture to 163° F without stirring, but brushing the inside of the saucepan with cold water to make the sugar crystals disappear. Take the pan off the stove and wait until the bubbles have almost completely disappeared.

Pour the mass onto the silicone mat. Flavor and dye the mass with the licorice aroma and food coloring. Using one or two dough scrapers, work the mass from the edges into the middle while it starts to thicken.

Divide the mass into three pieces. Put on the rubber gloves, then pull and fold each mass seven or eight times until it has thickened even more.

Pull and roll the mass into long, ½-inch-thick pieces and cut them into ½-inch-wide pieces with the oiled scissors. You have to work quickly here so the mass does not harden. Let the caramels harden on parchment paper, and then store them in airtight containers at room temperature.

Licorice Lollipops with Anise

If you choose, when you make these lollipops, you can skip dipping them in chocolate and adding the anise seeds. Sticks and lollipop molds are usually available at kitchenware stores or craft shops.

MAKES: 6–8 LOLLIPOPS

lollipop molds
1 tsp. neutral oil, like rapeseed or sunflower oil
lollipop sticks
3 tbsp. water
1⅙ cups cane sugar (8 oz.)
¼ cup + 2 tbsp. dextrose (2⅓ oz.)
4–5 drops licorice aroma or salty licorice aroma
4–5 drops black food coloring
1 tsp. whole anise seeds
3½ oz. dark chocolate, 70 %

Grease the molds with the oil and then place the sticks in them. Pour the water, cane sugar, and dextrose into a stainless steel, heavy-bottomed saucepan. Stir a few times to combine the ingredients. Boil the mixture to 323° F without stirring, but brush the inside of the saucepan with cold water to make the sugar crystals disappear.

Take the pan off the stove and wait until the bubbles have disappeared almost completely. Add the licorice aroma and food coloring while stirring, then fill the molds. Sprinkle with anise seeds and let the lollipops harden in the molds.

Chop and temper the chocolate (see directions below). Dip the lollipops partially into the chocolate and let the chocolate harden.

TEMPERING CHOCOLATE

Dark chocolate: Finely chop the chocolate, then heat two thirds of it to 122–131° F. Add the rest of the chocolate and stir until the temperature has cooled to 80–82° F. Then heat everything to the working temperature, 88–90° F.

Milk chocolate: Finely chop the chocolate, then heat two thirds of it to 113° F. Add the rest of the chocolate and stir until the temperature has cooled to 79–81° F. Then heat everything to the working temperature, 86° F.

Licorice Truffle Pralines

■ You can ask for chocolate shells in chocolate shops. If you can't get the shells, you can still make these truffles, just increase the dark chocolate by 2 oz. and leave the truffle mixture in the refrigerator overnight covered in plastic. Then, roll the mixture into balls and follow the instructions.

MAKES: 40 PIECES

7 oz. white chocolate
1 oz. dark chocolate, 56-70%
⅔ cup heavy cream
½ tsp. licorice granules
⅓ oz. glucose or honey
40 premade, dark chocolate shells
10 oz. dark chocolate, 64–70%

Licorice Sugar
⅔ cup cane sugar
1 tbsp. licorice granules

Cut up all of the chocolate and put it in a bowl. Boil the cream, licorice granules, and glucose. Pour the warm mixture over the chocolate and stir to a smooth truffle consistency. Fill a disposable piping bag with the mixture and let it cool.

Combine the cane sugar and licorice granules on a plate to make the licorice sugar.

Fill the chocolate shells with the truffle. Roll them in melted chocolate, and then immediately in the licorice sugar. Store them in airtight jars. They last for weeks at cool room temperature.

"A SILKY SMOOTH FILLING IN A CRUNCHY SHELL. GUARANTEED PLEASURE."

Salty Licorice Pralines

■ When making these delightful treats, use hard plastic molds if possible.

MAKES: 30–40 PIECES

Praline Shells

14 oz. dark chocolate, 56–70%, or milk
   chocolate

Truffle Filling

3½ oz. dark chocolate
3½ oz. milk chocolate
⅔ cup heavy cream
2 tbsp. glucose or honey
*3 tsp. salty licorice powder, optional: ½
   tsp. licorice granules and ½ tsp.
   salmiak salt*
⅔ oz. butter, room temperature

Cut up and temper the chocolate (see page 36 for directions). Carefully heat the molds with a heat gun or blow dryer and pour the chocolate into them. Tap the molds on the table a few times. Wait 30–60 seconds, then turn them upside down to let the excess chocolate pour out onto a piece of parchment paper. Let the shells harden at room temperature or in the refrigerator for about 10 minutes.

Chop all the chocolate for the filling and put it in a bowl. Boil the cream, glucose, and salty licorice powder. Pour the mixture into the bowl and stir until the chocolate has melted. Add the butter and blend it into a smooth truffle with a stick blender. Fill a disposable piping bag with the truffle filling. Let it rest for a couple of hours.

Fill the shells, then spread the tempered chocolate over them and leave the pralines at a cool room temperature for at least 6 hours. Turn the molds upside down and tap them carefully on the table until the chocolates come loose.

Licorice and Sesame Brittle

■ Good with ice cream. Or just as it is!

MAKES: 30–40 PIECES

1⅓ oz. butter
½ cup + 1 tbsp. cane sugar
1 tsp. licorice granules
⅔ cup sesame seeds
*optional: several drops of black food
   coloring*

Melt the butter in a heavy-bottomed saucepan over low heat. Add the sugar, raise the temperature slightly, and allow the sugar to melt. Add the licorice granules, sesame seeds, and, if desired, the food coloring. Stir.

Pour the mixture onto a baking sheet lined with a silicone mat or parchment paper. Place a piece of parchment paper over the top, then quickly roll it into a thin sheet. Remove the parchment paper and let it cool. Once it has cooled, break the brittle into pieces.

Soft Licorice Candy

■ Getting the correct measurements for the ingredients is important for this candy, so the weights are listed for this recipe. As a little twist for this recipe, you can slice the candy into 2-inch pieces, dip them in tempered chocolate (see page 36 for directions), and sprinkle with grated coconut or sea salt.

MAKES: 40 PIECES

10 sheets of gelatin
⅓ oz. licorice granules
⅛ oz. salty licorice powder
6 oz. water
⅓ oz. liquid malt or dark corn syrup
4½ oz. cane sugar
1½ oz. flour

Let the gelatin sheets soak in a large bowl of cold water for 5–10 minutes. Combine the rest of the ingredients in a saucepan, whisk briskly, and boil to 185° F, or until the mixture starts to thicken.

Remove the saucepan from the heat. Take the gelatin sheets out of the water, then place them in the saucepan and stir until they have melted. Let the mixture cool slightly.

Put the filling into a disposable piping bag with a ¼-inch round nozzle. Let the filling cool a little more, then pipe the mixture into long, round strips on a silicone mat. Let the pieces harden at room temperature for 2–4 days. After 1 or 2 days, turn the pieces over. The longer they are left, the harder and more viscous their texture will be. Cut the licorice into 1-inch-long pieces.

Store the candy in an airtight container at room temperature.

"A RECIPE FOR PREMIUM LICORICE. NOW YOU CAN FINALLY MAKE YOUR OWN!"

Salty Licorice Caramels—"Flames"

■ Making your own caramels requires a lot of practice, but it is very fun to try. You have to work pretty fast in order to cut the pieces before the caramel mass hardens. Note: the hot caramel mass should be handled by an adult or in the company of an adult.

MAKES: 150 CARAMELS

2–3 tbsp. sunflower or rapeseed oil
⅔ cup water
2⅓ cups cane sugar (16 oz.)
⅘ cup dextrose (4½ oz.)
6–8 drops liquid salty licorice aroma
black and red food coloring
salmiak salt
2–3 drops of neutral oil for the scissors

You will need one or two dough scrapers, a pair of scissors, a pair of rubber gloves, and a silicone mat.

Put a kitchen towel on a table, place a baking sheet on top, then put the silicone mat on the baking sheet. (If your silicone mat is thin, you can tape it to the edges of the sheet pan to stop it from moving.) Brush some oil on the silicone mat.

Stir together the water, cane sugar, and dextrose in a stainless steel saucepan.

Boil the mixture to 163° F without stirring, but brush the inside of the saucepan with cold water to make the sugar crystals disappear. Remove the pan from the heat and wait until the bubbles have almost completely disappeared.

Pour the mixture onto the silicone mat. (Note: if you have a marble countertop, you can oil the countertop and work directly on it.) Add the licorice aroma. Using the dough scrapers, work the mixture from the edges into the middle while it starts to thicken.

Divide the mass into three pieces. Dye two of the pieces black and the other one red (work with the scrapers). Put on the rubber gloves and pull and fold the pieces about seven or eight times until they thicken more. Cut the red mass into two pieces. Pull the smooth pieces into lengths and add a black piece to each red one. Pull and roll some more until the lengths are about ½ inch wide.

Cut the lengths into ½-inch-wide pieces with the oiled scissors. Let the caramels harden on parchment paper and sprinkle some salmiak salt onto them. Store the caramels at room temperature in an airtight container.

ICE CREAM

Licorice Ice Pops Dipped in White Chocolate

■ Popsicle molds can be found in department stores, craft shops, kitchenware stores, or online.

MAKES: 6 ICE POPS

½ batch of licorice ice cream (see the recipe on page 86)
popsicle mold
6 wooden popsicle sticks
3½ oz. white chocolate
1 tsp. licorice granules

Put the ice cream mixture into an ice cream maker until it reaches a thick and creamy texture (20–30 minutes). Fill a disposable piping bag with the ice cream mixture, then pipe it into the popsicle molds. Put a popsicle stick in each mold, then place in the freezer overnight.

Rinse the molds quickly in lukewarm water so the ice pops come loose. Put them on a small tray covered in plastic and put the tray in the freezer.

Finely chop the white chocolate and carefully melt it in the microwave. Remove the chocolate from the microwave periodically and stir it to ensure it does not burn.

Dip an ice pop into the white chocolate and immediately sprinkle some licorice granules over it. Work with one ice pop at a time and work quickly so the chocolate doesn't harden.

Enjoy the ice pops fresh, or put them in airtight packaging and store in the freezer.

"THE FLOWERS WERE FROZEN INTO A MOLD WITH HIGH EDGES."

Licorice Parfait

■ The leftover egg whites can be stored in the freezer for later, or, even better, they can be used for meringues, since meringues go well with this parfait. It can also be served with lightly whipped cream and sugared raspberries.

SERVINGS: 6–8

2 cups heavy cream
5 egg yolks
¼ cup + 2 tbsp. powdered sugar
1 tbsp. licorice granules or 2 tbsp.
　 licorice powder
3–4 tbsp. licorice syrup (see page 60)

Whip the cream. In a separate bowl, whip the egg yolks, powdered sugar, and licorice granules with a whisk until fluffy. Add the cream to the mixture.

Alternate layers of the ice cream mixture with layers of licorice syrup in a mold. Cover and place in the freezer for at least 5 hours.

If the parfait has been in the freezer for more than 5 hours, take it out 5–10 minutes before serving.

"TRY SERVING WITH GRATED DARK CHOCOLATE ON TOP. DELICIOUS AND SUPER EASY!"

Salty Licorice Ice Cream with Licorice Curd and Fresh Berries

■ To add some crunch to the ice cream, crush some chocolate cookies and sprinkle them on top. This recipe might make more curd than you need, but it's difficult to make a smaller batch. Any leftovers can be served with pancakes or waffles with vanilla ice cream and raspberries. Yummy!

SERVINGS: 6–8

Licorice Curd

½ tbsp. licorice granules or 1 tbsp.
  licorice powder
3 tbsp. water
1 cup cane sugar
1¾ oz. butter
2 eggs
optional: black food coloring

Salty Licorice Ice Cream

1 vanilla pod
1⅔ cups milk
1¼ cups heavy cream
1 tbsp. salty licorice powder
1 tbsp. licorice granules or licorice
  powder
6 egg yolks
¾ cup cane sugar
fresh berries, black raspberries, blackberries, or blueberries

To make the curd, mix the licorice gran-ules and water in a stainless steel saucepan. Stir and bring to a boil. Add about ¼ cup of the sugar and the butter and stir while it melts. Remove the pan from the stove. Whisk the eggs and remaining sugar together and stir it into the saucepan. While whisking briskly, heat to 185° F or until the curd starts to thicken. Let the curd cool completely in a bath of cold water. If desired, add some black food coloring. Place the curd in the refrigerator.

To make the ice cream, split the vanilla pod lengthwise. Seed and put the seeds and the pod in a heavy-bottomed saucepan with the milk, cream, salty licorice powder, and licorice granules. Stir and bring the mixture to a boil, then remove the saucepan from the heat.

In a large bowl, whip the egg yolks and sugar with a whisk until light and fluffy. Remove the vanilla pod from the saucepan, then pour the warm mixture into the bowl. Whisk until smooth, then pour the mixture back into the saucepan. While whisking briskly, heat the mixture to 185° F or until the curd starts to thicken.

Strain the mixture into a bowl and cool it in a bath of cold water. Cover the bowl with plastic and leave it in the refrigerator for a few hours. Then put the mixture into an ice cream maker and run it until it reaches a thick and creamy texture (20–30 minutes).

Put the ice cream mixture into a mold while rippling it with the licorice curd. Cover in plastic and freeze for at least 1 hour.

Top the ice cream with the fresh berries and serve the remaining curd in a bowl on the side.

Licorice Root and Apple Sorbet with Fennel Topping

■ A refreshing and thrilling sorbet—and it's filled with vitamins! This can also be used as an entremet.

SERVINGS: 10

Sorbet

1 sheet of gelatin
¼ cup + 2 tbsp. water
1 tbsp. ground licorice root
½ tsp. fennel seeds or anise seeds, ground with a pestle and mortar
1 cup cane sugar
2 tbsp. glucose or honey
2 ⅓ cups apple purée (4–5 green apples, cored and blended)
2 tbsp. lime juice

Fennel Topping

½ fennel
1 green apple
½ lemon, zest and juice
1 tbsp. honey
fresh herbs for garnish (e.g., wild yarrow, thyme, oregano, mint)

For the sorbet, soak the gelatin sheet in a bath of cold water for 5–10 minutes. Combine the water, ground licorice root, fennel seeds, sugar, and glucose in a saucepan and bring to a boil. Remove the pan from the stove, take the gelatin sheet out of the water and add it to the warm syrup. Stir until the gelatin sheet melts, then let the syrup cool.

Mix the apple purée and lime juice together in a bowl. Whisk the cooled syrup into the bowl, then put the mixture into an ice cream maker for 20–30 minutes, until it reaches a smooth texture.

To make the fennel topping, thinly slice the fennel and apple. Combine the slices with the lemon juice, lemon zest, and honey.

Dish out the sorbet in bowls, top with the fennel topping, and garnish with herbs.

If the sorbet will not be immediately served, it can be covered and stored in the freezer.

Ice Pops with Licorice and Cherries

■ Prettier popsicles than these are hard to find! The licorice/cherry combination is a real hit, and the creamy texture is a plus. Why not serve these popsicles as a dessert, preferably with iced berries?

MAKES: 6 POPSICLES

½ vanilla pod
¾ cup milk
½ cup heavy cream
3 egg yolks
¼ cup + 2 tbsp. cane sugar
2 tsp. licorice granules or 3 tsp. licorice powder
½ cup cherry or black currant purée
6 licorice roots or wooden popsicle sticks

Split the vanilla pod lengthwise, seed it, then put the pod and seeds into a heavy-bottomed saucepan with the milk and cream. Stir and bring to a boil, then remove the saucepan from the stove.

With a whisk, whip the yolks, sugar, and licorice granules to a fluffy foam. Add the warm milk mixture and whisk until smooth. Pour the mixture back into the saucepan. Stir and heat to 185° F or until it starts to thicken.

Strain the mixture into a bowl and cool it in a bath of cold water. Leave the bowl in the refrigerator until the mixture is really cold. Add the berry purée, but save a few tablespoons for the popsicle molds.

Put the mixture into the ice cream maker until it reaches a thick and creamy texture (20–30 minutes). Pour the mixture into a disposable piping bag and pipe it into the popsicle molds. Add some purée in layers to make the popsicle look marbled. Put a licorice root or wooden stick into each mold, then put them in the freezer overnight or until serving.

Rinse the molds quickly in lukewarm water so the popsicles come loose. Serve as they are or put them on a small tray covered with plastic and leave them in the freezer for another hour.

Tip!
To make iced berries, simply spread fresh berries out on a sheet pan and place in the freezer.

Licorice Frozen Yogurt with Black Currants

■ Tart, sweet, cold, and the wonderfully full-bodied flavors of black currant and licorice combine for this taste-pleasing experience!

SERVINGS: 8–10

1 sheet of gelatin
⅔ cup water
1 cup cane sugar
1½ oz. glucose or honey
1 tbsp. licorice granules
1½ cups yogurt
1¼ cups black currant purée

Let the gelatin sheet soak in a bowl of cold water for 5–10 minutes. Combine the water, sugar, glucose, and licorice granules in a saucepan. Bring to a boil and stir until the sugar has melted. Remove the pan from the stove. Take the gelatin sheet out of the water and add it to the warm syrup. Stir until the sheet has melted, then let the syrup cool completely.

Mix the yogurt and black currant purée into the syrup. Put the mixture into an ice cream maker for approximately 20–30 minutes until it reaches a solid and creamy consistency. Place in a container and cover with plastic or a lid and place in the freezer for at least 1 hour before serving.

"A FRESH ICE CREAM WITH THRILLING FLAVORS. GOES WELL WITH A GLASS OF CHAMPAGNE."

Ice Cream Toppings

Licorice Caramel Sauce with Licorice Butterscotch

SERVINGS: 8

1 cup heavy cream
¼ cup + 2 tbsp. cane sugar
¼ cup + 2 tbsp. golden syrup
about ⅔ oz. licorice butterscotch

Stir the cream, sugar, and syrup together in a saucepan. Cut the licorice butterscotch into small pieces and put them into the saucepan. While stirring, bring the sauce to a gentle boil. Allow sauce to simmer for about 10 minutes while continuing to stir.

Licorice Caramel Sauce
A good base recipe. The sauce thickens once it has cooled off.

SERVINGS: 6–8

¼ cup + 2 tbsp. golden syrup
¼ cup + 2 tbsp. cane sugar
¼ cup + 2 tbsp. heavy cream
2 tsp. licorice granules
optional: black food coloring

Combine the syrup, sugar, cream, and licorice granules in a saucepan. If desired, add the food coloring. While stirring, bring the mixture to a boil, and let it continue to boil until it reaches a temperature of 240–245° F, or until the sauce starts to thicken. Remove the pan from the heat and allow the sauce to cool.

Licorice Syrup
This syrup is good for waffles and pancakes, and is even better when combined with raspberry or cloudberry jam.

MAKES: ABOUT ⅔ CUP

2 tbsp. water
1 tbsp. licorice granules
½ cup dark corn syrup
optional: 3–4 drops salty licorice aroma or anise
optional: black food coloring

Pour the water into a small saucepan, then add the licorice granules and let them dissolve in the water. Next, add the syrup and bring to a boil. Let the syrup boil for a few minutes, then remove from the heat. Add the salty licorice aroma and food coloring if desired. If necessary, remove any skin from the top of the pan. Let the syrup cool, then pour it into a bottle with a cap.

Licorice and Raspberry Eton Mess
You can make a delicious eton mess by breaking pieces of flat licorice meringues (see the recipe on page 86) and serving with raspberry sorbet or vanilla ice cream, fresh raspberries, and licorice caramel sauce.

Warm Licorice Milk
Made by quickly stirring 2 tbsp. of the Licorice Syrup into a cup of warm milk. Want some added luxury? Spike it with whiskey, then top with whipped cream and grated dark chocolate.

PASTRIES

Macarons

■ In some recipes there's a fine line between success and failure when baking these, so I've decided to state the main ingredients by weight to make the recipe more precise. You can choose whether you want to use regular licorice powder or salty licorice powder.

MAKES: 20–24 MACARONS

Macarons

2 oz. egg whites, room temperature (about 1 ½)
2 tbsp. cane sugar
3 ½ oz. powdered sugar
1 ¾ oz. almond flour
1 tsp. licorice powder or salty licorice powder
black food coloring in powder form and as paste

Buttercream Filling

3 ½ oz. butter, room temperature
3 ½ tbsp. powdered sugar
2 tsp. licorice or salty licorice powder
1 egg yolk

Put the egg white in a bowl, then cover the bowl with plastic and let it sit overnight at room temperature.

Combine the almond flour and powdered sugar in a blender until it's a fine powder. NOTE: Do not blend for too long or the almond oil will make the mixture sticky.

Put the egg white in a clean, dry bowl. Using an electric mixer, blend until it turns foamy. While continuing to mix, add the sugars 1 tablespoon at a time. Continue mixing until the meringue turns stiff and shiny. Gently fold in the almond flour, licorice powder, and food coloring.

Fill a disposable piping bag with the meringue and use a round nozzle to pipe circles on a baking sheet lined with parchment paper. They will increase in size when you bake them, so be sure to leave space between them on the baking sheet. Let them stand and rest for 1 hour before baking.

Set the oven to 300° F. Bake the cookies in the middle of the oven for 12–14 minutes. Keep an eye on them to ensure that they do not burn. If necessary, move the baking sheet to a lower rack in the oven. Gently push down on one of the cookies; if it releases from the paper, they are ready. Remove the baking sheet from the oven and let them cool.

Beat the butter for the filling, then add the powdered sugar and licorice powder. Add the egg yolk while mixing.

Fill a disposable piping bag with the buttercream, pipe some filling onto half of the cookies, then place another cookie half on top. Stored in an airtight container, they will keep fresh for at least a few days. They can also be stored for a longer period in an airtight container in the freezer.

Chocolate and Licorice Cake

■ A tasty chocolate cake with a nice licorice accent. Serve with fresh berries, whipped cream, or vanilla ice cream.

SERVINGS: 8

Chocolate Cake
butter and fine breadcrumbs for the pan
3 eggs
1¼ cups cane sugar
2 tsp. vanilla sugar
¾ cup flour
¼ cup + 2 tbsp. cocoa powder
2 tsp. baking powder
¼ cup + 2 tbsp. milk

Chocolate and Licorice Filling
5⅓ oz. dark chocolate, 56–64%
½ cup heavy cream
3 tsp. licorice powder or 2 tsp. licorice granules
1½ tbsp. glucose or golden syrup
1⅜ oz. butter, room temperature

Ganache
7 oz. dark chocolate
¾ cup heavy cream
1½ oz. butter, room temperature

Garnish
macarons (see recipe on page 64), optional: Oreos
fresh cherries, raspberries, or blackberries
optional: licorice powder or licorice granules

Preheat the oven to 350° F. Grease and crumb an 8-inch-diameter pan that is at least 3 inches deep.

Using a whisk, whip together the eggs, cane sugar, and vanilla sugar in a bowl until light and fluffy. In a separate bowl, combine the flour, cocoa powder, and baking powder. Heat the milk to just below boiling, then add it to the egg mixture. Fold in the dry ingredients and mix until smooth.

Pour the batter into the pan and bake for approximately 50 minutes, or until the cake is baked through. Leave the cake in the pan for a few minutes, then turn it over on a plate. Let the cake cool completely, then slice it into three layers with a serrated knife.

Chop the chocolate for the filling and set it aside in a bowl. Boil the cream, licorice powder, and glucose in a saucepan. Whisk until the licorice has dissolved. Next, pour the cream over the chocolate and stir until the chocolate has melted. Allow the mixture to cool to about 110° F, then add the butter and mix, preferably with a stick blender. Put one cake section on a plate and spread half of the filling over it. Add the second cake layer on top and spread on the remaining filling. Cover with the final cake layer.

Chop the chocolate for the ganache, put it in a bowl, and set it aside. Boil the cream, then pour it over the chocolate and stir until the chocolate has melted. Add the butter, a little at a time, and whisk or blend until it has melted. Let the ganache cool slightly, then cover the cake with it. Let the ganache harden in the refrigerator. Garnish the cake with macarons and/or berries. If desired, add some licorice powder.

Rhubarb Cake with Licorice Meringue

■ If you choose, you can skip the meringue and serve with licorice ice cream instead (see the recipe on page 86).

SERVINGS: 12

Shortcrust Pastry Bottom
7 oz. cold butter
½ cup cane sugar
2 cups flour

Rhubarb Filling
7 oz. almond paste
3½ oz. butter, room temperature
2 eggs, separated
1 whole egg
2 tbsp. flour
3 tbsp. cane sugar
7 oz. rhubarb (1–2 stems) plus some extra
* for garnish*

Licorice Meringue Topping
2 oz. egg whites (1½ eggs)
3½ oz. cane sugar
1½ oz. water
1 tsp. licorice granules or 2 tsp. licorice
* powder plus some extra for garnish*
optional: white or red currants for garnish

Cut up the butter for the shortcrust pastry and combine it with the sugar in a bowl. Add the flour and blend quickly into a dough. Cover the dough in plastic, then place it in the refrigerator for 1 hour.

Preheat the oven to 365° F. Grease a 9-inch springform pan. Roll out the dough and then place it into the pan. Cut off any dough that hangs over the edge of the pan. Prick the dough on the bottom of the pan with a fork. Then place the pan in the refrigerator.

Finely grate the almond paste and put it in a bowl. Mix in the butter. Whisk together the egg yolks and the egg. Add the flour. In a separate bowl, whisk the egg whites then add the sugar and whisk into a meringue. Add the meringue to the batter. Cut the rhubarb into pieces (only trim the rougher stems) and mix into the batter. Pour the batter into the pan and bake in the middle of the oven for 40 minutes. Move the cake to an oven rack that is one level lower and bake for another 5–10 minutes, until the filling has set. Let the cake cool completely.

Put the egg white for the meringue topping in a bowl. Mix the sugar and water in a saucepan. Boil the mixture to 230° F, meanwhile whisk the egg whites to a stiff foam. Keep boiling the liquid until it reaches 250° F. Pour it directly into the egg whites in a thin stream while whisking. Keep whisking until the meringue has cooled. Sprinkle with the licorice granules and work it evenly into the meringue. Spread the meringue over the cake and carefully brown it with a propane torch.

Garnish with rhubarb and currants. Sprinkle with some licorice granules or licorice powder if desired.

Tip!
Rhubarb spirals: "Peel" the rhubarb with a cheese slicer. Put the slices in very cold water in the refrigerator for 1 hour. Remove the slices from the water and let them dry on some kitchen towels.

Licorice Sponge Cake with Orange

■ This sponge cake has a nice, mild taste of licorice and orange. For a more intensive licorice flavor, slightly increase the amount of licorice. But be careful—too much will make it bitter.

SERVINGS: 12

butter and fine breadcrumbs to prepare the pan
3½ oz. butter
½ cup + 1 tbsp. milk
3 eggs
1¼ cups cane sugar
2 cups flour
1 tbsp. vanilla sugar
2 tsp. baking powder
2 tsp. licorice granules or 3 tsp. licorice powder
1 orange, zested

Preheat the oven to 350° F. Grease and crumb a sponge cake pan.

Melt the butter then add the milk. Using a whisk, whip the eggs and sugar together in a bowl until fluffy, then add them to the butter mixture. Mix the dry ingredients together in a separate bowl, then combine them to the batter and add the orange zest.

Pour the batter into the pan and bake in the middle of the oven for 45–50 minutes. Use a cake tester in the center of the cake. If it comes out dry, then the cake is done.

Remove the cake from the oven and let it sit for a few minutes. Turn the pan upside down onto a plate. Let the cake cool completely before removing the pan.

Licorice Meringues

■ There's something special about licorice meringues. The taste is hard to describe . . . you have to try them for yourself!

MAKES: 20 PIECES

5⅓ oz. egg whites (about 4)

1⅙ cups cane sugar

2–3 tsp. licorice granules, licorice powder, or salty licorice powder

½–1 tbsp. licorice syrup (see the recipe on page 60)

optional: black food coloring

extra licorice granules, licorice powder, or salty licorice powder to sprinkle on top

Preheat the oven to 270° F. Mix the egg whites and sugar together in a stainless steel bowl.

Place the bowl over a pan of water and heat the mixture to 130–140° F while whisking. Remove the bowl from the pan and continue mixing the meringue with an electric mixer until it cools.

Sprinkle with some licorice granules, drizzle with some licorice syrup, and add a few drops of food coloring if you like. Fold the batter several times until it looks nice and marbled.

Drop the batter by rounded teaspoonful onto a baking sheet lined with parchment paper. Sprinkle with some licorice granules, then bake for 35–40 minutes. The meringues should be a bit sticky in the center.

Store in a dry, airtight container.

"CRUNCHY AND CHEWY MERINGUES THAT TASTE GOOD WITH A CUP OF COFFEE OR A SCOOP OF ICE CREAM."

Licorice Chocolate Cake

■ Of course I want a chocolate cake recipe in my book . . . or maybe even two—both with wonderful, creamy glazes.

SERVINGS: 10

Cake
butter and flour for the pan
3½ oz. butter
2 eggs
1¼ cups cane sugar
2 tsp. licorice granules
¾ cup flour
4 tbsp. cocoa powder
1 tsp. vanilla sugar
¼ tsp. salt

Glaze
2⅔ oz. dark chocolate, 70%
⅓ cup heavy cream
1 tsp. licorice granules
optional: licorice granules for garnish

Preheat the oven to 400° F. Grease and flour a 9-inch springform pan.

Melt the butter. Combine the eggs, sugar, and licorice granules together. Add the butter and stir to combine. Next, add all the dry ingredients and mix thoroughly.

Pour the batter into the pan and bake on a rack set at the lowest level in the oven for 15–17 minutes. Let the cake cool for about 1 hour so that it sets properly.

Cut up the chocolate for the glaze. Put the cream and licorice granules into a saucepan and bring to a boil. Remove the pan from the heat, then add the chocolate and stir until it melts. Allow the glaze to cool then drizzle it over the cake. If desired, sprinkle some licorice granules over the cake once the glaze has hardened.

"HERE ARE THE RECIPES FOR TWO DELICIOUS CHOCOLATE CAKES. IT'S IMPOSSIBLE TO PICK A FAVORITE!"

White Chocolate Cake with Lime Marinated Berries

■ Want some more licorice flavor? Simply let a licorice root boil with the syrup for the berries.

SERVINGS: 12–14

Cake
butter and fine breadcrumbs for the pan
8 oz. white chocolate
10 oz. butter
3 eggs
1 cup cane sugar
2 tbsp. cognac or whiskey
1 tbsp. licorice granules or 2 tbsp. licorice powder
¾ cup flour

White Chocolate Glaze
5⅓ oz. white chocolate
3 tbsp. heavy cream
fresh berries for garnish
1 tsp. licorice granules or licorice powder

Lime Marinated Berries
¼ cup + 2 tbsp. water
3 tbsp. cane sugar
1 tbsp. honey
optional: 1 licorice root
1 lime, finely grated zest and juice
2 pints mixed berries, such as raspberries, blackberries, and blueberries

Preheat the oven to 440° F. Grease and crumb a 10-inch springform pan.

Finely chop the white chocolate. Melt the butter in a saucepan, then remove the pan from the heat. Add the white chocolate and stir until it has melted. Using a whisk, whip the eggs and sugar in a bowl until fluffy. Add the chocolate mixture, cognac, licorice, and flour and stir into a smooth batter.

Pour the batter into the pan and bake for approximately 30 minutes on a rack set at the lowest level in the oven. Remove the pan from the oven and let the cake cool. Place it in the refrigerator for a couple of hours until it has set.

Finely chop the white chocolate for the glaze and put it in a bowl. Boil the cream in a saucepan, then pour it over the white chocolate and stir until all the chocolate has melted. Let the glaze cool, then spread it over the cake and let it harden. Garnish with fresh berries and sprinkle with licorice granules just before serving.

In a stainless steel saucepan, bring the water, sugar, and honey to a boil. If desired, add the licorice root. Remove the saucepan from the heat and stir in the lime zest and juice. Let the syrup cool, then carefully mix the berries into it. Serve the berries with the cake.

Licorice Doughnuts with Rhubarb Dip

■ The combination of licorice and rhubarb is absolutely superb. Use caution when deep–frying on the stove.

MAKES: 60 DOUGHNUTS

Doughnuts

1¾ oz. yeast
5⅓ oz. butter
2 cups milk
½ cup cane sugar
½ tsp. salt
6½ cups flour
2 tsp. licorice granules
1¼ cups cane sugar
2 tbsp. licorice granules
about 3 cups neutral oil for deep-frying,
  preferably corn or sunflower oil

Rhubarb Dip

3 rhubarb stems
3–4 tbsp. water
1 vanilla pod
½ cup cane sugar

licorice syrup (see the recipe on page
  60) and vanilla ice cream to serve with

Crumble the yeast into a dough mixer or bowl. Melt the butter in a saucepan, stir in the milk and heat to 98° F. Pour the liquid mixture over the yeast and stir to combine. Add ½ cup sugar, salt, and half of the flour into the mixture and combine. Then add the licorice granules and the remaining flour. Work into a smooth dough, about 5 minutes in a dough blender or 10 minutes by hand.

Place the dough onto a floured surface then roll it to a ½-inch thickness. Punch doughnuts from the dough using a biscuit or doughnut cutter. If using a biscuit cutter, make a small hole in the center of each doughnut. Let the doughnuts rise for about 10 minutes.

Mix 1¼ cups of cane sugar and 2 tablespoons of licorice granules on a tray or on a large, deep plate.

Heat the oil to 320-340° F in a large saucepan. Keep a lid close by in case of fire. Deep-fry two or three doughnuts at a time until they turn golden brown, which takes a couple of minutes. As they're cooking, turn the doughnuts several times. Using a slotted spoon, scoop the doughnuts out of the oil, allow excess oil to drain off, then dip them directly into the licorice sugar, ensuring both sides are covered, then place them on a rack or sheet of parchment paper to cool.

Clean and cut the rhubarb for the dip into small pieces. Peel the larger stalks first. Put the pieces in a stainless steel saucepan and add the water. Split the vanilla pod lengthwise and seed it. Put the pod and seeds into the saucepan. Bring to a boil and allow it to boil for 5 minutes. Add the sugar and boil for another 5 minutes. Let it cool, then remove the vanilla pod.

Serve the doughnuts with rhubarb dip, licorice syrup, and vanilla ice cream.

Licorice Tosca Rolls

■ Tasty rolls with a licorice and almond paste filling and a tosca glaze on top. Impossible to mistake these for anything but the best!

MAKES: 30 ROLLS

Rolls
1¾ oz. yeast
¾ cup milk
6 oz. butter, room temperature
1 egg
3 tbsp. simple syrup or cane sugar
½ tsp. salt
3½–4 cups flour

Licorice and Almond Paste Filling
2⅔ oz. almond paste
3½ oz. butter, room temperature
1 tbsp. cane sugar
1 tbsp. brown sugar
½ tbsp. licorice granules or 1 tbsp. licorice powder

Tosca Glaze
1¾ oz. butter
⅔ cup cane sugar
1 tbsp. milk
1 tbsp. flour
1 tsp. licorice granules or 2 tsp. licorice powder
1¾ oz. almond flakes

Crumble the yeast into a dough mixer or bowl. Heat the milk to 98° F, then stir in the butter, egg, syrup, and salt. Add the flour a little at a time until the dough is smooth. Work the dough for 5 minutes in the machine or 10 minutes by hand. Cover the bowl with a kitchen towel and let the dough rise for 40 minutes.

Finely grate the almond paste for the filling and combine it with the butter, cane sugar, brown sugar, and licorice granules.

Place the dough on a floured work surface and divide it into two pieces. Roll one piece into a rectangle, about 18 x 12 inches, then spread half of the filling over the dough and roll it up. Slice the dough into 1-inch-thick pieces and put the pieces into paper liners on a baking sheet. Repeat the procedure with the other piece of dough. Cover the dough with a kitchen towel and let it rise for 30–40 minutes. While the dough is rising, preheat the oven to 480° F.

Combine all of the ingredients for the glaze in a saucepan over low-medium heat and stir gently until the butter has melted. Cover the rolls with the glaze and bake them in the middle of the oven for 8–10 minutes. Let them cool on a rack.

Licorice Biscotti

■ Tasty little biscuits that go well with a cup of tea or coffee. They also taste good with a rich red wine, such as Malbec or Amarone. The licorice caramel seeps out a little while baking, but hardens again after cooling.

MAKES: 50 PIECES

3½ oz. butter, room temperature
¾ cup cane sugar
3 eggs
2½ cups flour
1 tsp. vanilla sugar
1 tsp. baking powder
¼ tsp. salt
1 tbsp. licorice granules or licorice powder
4½ oz. dark chocolate, 64–70%
⅔ oz. licorice toffee
¾ cup almonds
1 egg white for brushing
3 tbsp. raw sugar

Preheat the oven to 350° F. Mix the butter, sugar, eggs, flour, baking powder, salt, and licorice together in a bowl. Cut up the chocolate and work it into the dough. Cut the toffee into little pieces and chop the almonds into big pieces, then mix them into the dough.

Divide the dough into three pieces and roll them out so they are the same length as the baking sheet. Place the pieces of dough onto the baking sheet lined with parchment paper, brush with egg whites, then sprinkle with the raw sugar. Bake for 20–25 minutes. Remove the pan from the oven and let the biscotti cool for 10 minutes. Lower the oven temperature to 300° F.

Slice the biscotti diagonally into ½-inch-thick pieces. Put the biscotti on a baking sheet and let them dry in the oven for 10 minutes. Turn off the heat, but leave the biscotti in the oven for another 10 minutes. Remove from the oven, let them cool completely, and then store them in an airtight container.

DESSERT

Tiny Licorice Caramel Pies à la Snickers

■ Everyone who has tasted these little pies agrees: they are delicious! The single-serving size makes them even more fun.

SERVINGS: 8
Shortcrust Pastry Bottom
7 oz. cold butter
½ cup cane sugar
about 2 cups flour
about 2 cups dried peas (to keep the edges in place in the pie pans)

Licorice Caramel Filling
5⅓ oz. butter
¼ cup + 2 tbsp. cane sugar
¼ cup + 2 tbsp. golden syrup
¼ cup + 2 tbsp. heavy cream
1 tbsp. cocoa powder
1 tbsp. licorice granules
optional: black food coloring

½ cup salted peanuts

Milk Chocolate Glaze
3½ oz. milk chocolate
⅓ cup heavy cream
1 tsp. golden syrup
1 tsp. butter, room temperature

Cut the butter for the shortcrust pastry into cubes and combine it with the sugar in a bowl. Add the flour and quickly knead into a smooth dough. You can also mix the ingredients with a blender. Put the dough in a plastic bag and place it in the refrigerator for 1 hour.

Preheat the oven to 365° F and grease eight small pie pans, about 3 inches in diameter. Roll out the dough and then line the pans with it. Use a knife to slice off any dough that hangs over the edge of the pans. Prick the dough on the bottom of the pans with a fork. Cover the bottom of each crust with dried peas then bake for 10–12 minutes. Remove the pans from the oven and let them cool completely, then remove the peas.

Melt the butter for the caramel filling in a saucepan. Add the sugar, syrup, cream, cocoa powder, and licorice granules. Carefully boil the mixture to 250° F. Stir occasionally to ensure the bottom does not burn. If desired, add a few drops of food coloring. Pour the caramel filling into the crusts and let it cool. Next, divide the peanuts into the pies.

Finely chop the milk chocolate for the glaze and put it in a bowl. Boil the cream and syrup, then pour it over the chocolate. Stir until all of the chocolate has melted. Add the butter and stir. Drizzle the glaze over the pies and let it harden before serving.

Licorice Ice Cream with Flat Licorice Meringues

■ These meringues are very easy to make—just whisk together and spread them out on a tray.

SERVINGS: 6–8

Licorice Ice Cream
1 vanilla pod
1⅔ cups milk
1¼ cups heavy cream
1 tbsp. licorice granules or 2 tbsp. licorice powder
6 egg yolks
¾ cup cane sugar

Licorice Meringues
(makes 2 sheets)
2 oz. egg whites (1½ eggs)
½ tsp. lemon juice
3 tbsp. cane sugar
¼ cup + 2 tbsp. powdered sugar
1 tsp. licorice granules or 2 tsp. licorice powder

½ batch licorice syrup (see the recipe on page 60) to serve with
sorrel, extra licorice granules and optional: crumbs of raspberry meringue (see the recipe on page 94) for garnish

Split the vanilla pod lengthwise, scrape out the seeds, then put the pod and seeds in a heavy-bottomed saucepan with the milk, cream, and licorice granules. Boil while stirring, then remove the pan from the stove.

Using a whisk, whip the egg yolks and sugar together in a bowl until fluffy.

Remove the vanilla pod, then pour the hot liquids into the bowl. Whisk into a smooth batter, then pour it back into the saucepan. While stirring, heat to 185° F, or until the mixture starts to thicken.

Strain the mixture into a bowl and cool it in a bath of cold water. Cover the bowl with plastic and let it cool in the refrigerator for a few hours. Then put the mixture into an ice cream maker for 20–30 minutes. Leave in the freezer until serving.

Preheat the oven to 300° F. Whisk the egg whites and lemon juice for the meringues into a foam. Reduce the speed of the electric mixer and add half of the sugar, mixing until it's fully combined. Add the remaining sugar, increase the speed, and mix for a couple of minutes. Sift together the powdered sugar and licorice and fold it into the meringue with a rubber spatula.

Divide the meringue evenly onto two baking sheets lined with parchment paper, then spread the meringue out thinly. Bake for 3–4 minutes, then lower the temperature to 210° F and continue baking for about 1 hour. Allow the meringue to cool on the trays then break it into pieces.

Put pieces of meringue onto plates, put some licorice ice cream on them, and garnish with sorrel, licorice granules, and, if desired, raspberry meringue crumbs. Drizzle some licorice syrup over the ice cream and serve. Tastes good paired with some sweet Malbec, port, or Madeira wine.

Tiny Licorice Caramel Pies with Blueberry Meringues

■ For this recipe, the meringue ingredients are provided by weight for a better result.

SERVINGS: 8

Shortcrust Pastry Bottom

7 oz. cold butter
½ cup cane sugar
about 2 cups flour
about 2 cups dried peas (to keep the edges in place in the pie pans)

Licorice Caramel Filling

5⅓ oz. butter
3⅓ oz. cane sugar
3⅓ oz. golden syrup
3⅓ oz. heavy cream
1 tbsp. cocoa powder
1 tsp. vanilla sugar
1 tbsp. licorice granules
optional: black food coloring

Blueberry Meringue

2 oz. egg whites (1½ eggs)
3⅓ oz. cane sugar
1¼ oz. water
1½ oz. blueberry purée (blended fresh or frozen and thawed blueberries)
about 3½ oz. fresh blueberries for garnish
optional: licorice granules to sprinkle on top

Cut the butter for the crust and combine it with the sugar in a bowl. Add the flour and quickly knead into a smooth dough. You can also mix the ingredients in a food processor. Place the dough in a plastic bag and put it in the refrigerator for 1 hour.

Preheat the oven to 365° F. Grease eight 3-inch pie pans. Roll out the dough then line each pan. Use a knife to cut off any dough that hangs over the edge, then prick the bottom of each crust with a fork. Fill the bottom of the pan with dried peas and bake the crusts for 10–12 minutes. Take the pans out of the oven and let them cool completely. Remove the peas.

Melt the butter for the caramel filling in a saucepan. Add the sugar, syrup, cream, cocoa powder, vanilla sugar, and licorice granules. Carefully boil the mixture to 250° F. Stir occasionally to ensure the bottom does not burn. Add some food coloring if desired. Pour the caramel filling into the crusts and let it cool.

Put the egg whites for the meringue into a bowl. Combine the sugar, water, and blueberry purée in a saucepan. Boil the mixture to 230° F, then whisk the egg whites into a stiff foam. Keep boiling the mixture to 250° F, then immediately pour a thin stream of it into the egg white while whisking. Continue whisking until the meringue has cooled.

Immediately fill a piping bag with a ½-inch round nozzle and pipe little dollops onto the pies. (If the meringue feels a bit stiff, just whisk it by hand a little until it becomes soft again.) If you want, you can brown the tops of the meringue drops with a propane torch. Add some fresh blueberries and sprinkle on the licorice granules.

Licorice Ice Cream Cake with Nectarines and Passion Fruit Curd

■ If you want a stronger licorice flavor in the ice cream, just increase the licorice granules by 1 teaspoon before freezing.

SERVINGS: 12

Bottom Crust
2 oz. butter
12–15 graham crackers (5 ⅓ oz.)
1 tbsp. cocoa powder

Passion Fruit Curd
½ sheet of gelatin
1 lemon, juiced
2 passion fruits
¼ cup + 2 tbsp. cane sugar
1 ¼ oz. butter
1 egg
1 egg yolk

Licorice Ice Cream
1 ⅔ cups heavy cream
4 yolks + 1 egg white
¼ cup + 2 tbsp. cane sugar
2 tsp. licorice granules or 3 tsp. licorice powder
nectarine slices and mint leaves for garnish
licorice syrup or caramel sauce to serve with (see the recipes on page 60)

Melt the butter. Use a food processor to make the crackers into fine crumbs. Add the cocoa powder and butter and mix together. Spread the crust into an 8-inch springform pan and flatten with the back of a spoon. Put the pan in the refrigerator.

Let the gelatin for the curd soak in a bowl of cold water for 5–10 minutes. Pour the lemon juice into a stainless steel saucepan. Split the passion fruits and scrape the seeds into the saucepan. Add the sugar and butter, then put the pan on the stove and melt the butter. Stir the mixture and remove the pan from the stove. Whisk the egg and yolk in a bowl, then add to the saucepan while stirring vigorously. Put the pan back onto the stove and whisk until the curd starts to thicken. Do not let it boil! Take the gelatin sheet out of the water and place it in the warm curd. Stir until the sheet melts. Let the curd cool completely.

Whip up the cream for the ice cream. Whip the yolks, sugar, and licorice granules to a fluffy foam. In a separate bowl, whisk the egg white to a stiff foam. Fold the cream into the yolk mixture, then add the egg white.

Pour half of the mixture into the springform pan, then put it in the freezer for 30 minutes. Drizzle on the curd, then add the rest of the ice cream mixture. Leave the cake in the freezer for 5–6 hours. Remove the cake from the freezer and allow it to rest 5–10 minutes before serving. Garnish the cake with the nectarine slices and mint and serve with licorice syrup or licorice caramel sauce.

If you intend to leave the cake in the freezer for a longer period of time, cover it with plastic once it has frozen.

Belgian Licorice Waffles with Licorice Syrup

■ In Belgium, you can buy waffles at street or beach stalls. They are served with myriads of toppings, such as whipped cream, ice cream, sauces, and jams.

MAKES: 12 WAFFLES

2 eggs
5½ oz. butter
1 cup milk
¾ cup water or soda water
½ oz. yeast
⅓ cup cane sugar
2 tsp. vanilla sugar
½ tsp. salt
3 cups flour
*2 tsp. licorice granules or 3 tsp. licorice
  powder*
melted butter to brush the waffle iron with
*vanilla ice cream, licorice syrup (see the
  recipe on page 60), or maple syrup to
  serve with*

Separate the eggs. Put the egg whites in a clean, dry bowl.

Melt the butter, then add the milk and water and heat to 98° F. Crumble the yeast into a bowl and pour the liquid over it. Add the egg yolks, sugar, vanilla sugar, salt, flour, and licorice. Stir into a smooth batter.

Whisk the egg whites and fold them into the batter. Let the batter rest for 20 minutes, then cook using a Belgian waffle iron. Brush the iron with melted butter between waffles.

Serve immediately with vanilla ice cream, licorice syrup, or maple syrup. Goes very well with sugared raspberries (see the recipe below) or warm cloudberry jam.

Sugared Raspberries
1 pint raspberries
1–2 tbsp. cane sugar

Put the raspberries in a bowl, cover with the sugar and let sit for 1 hour. Stir until the sugar has melted.

"USE A BELGIAN WAFFLE IRON, IF YOU CAN FIND ONE, TO MAKE NICE, THICK WAFFLES, BUT A REGULAR WAFFLE IRON WORKS JUST AS WELL."

White Chocolate Mousse with Licorice

■ A heavenly smooth mousse that melts in your mouth. The little jolt of licorice is the perfect finishing touch. Just remember that the mousse needs about 12 hours in the refrigerator.

SERVINGS: 6

White Chocolate Mousse

3½ oz. white chocolate

1 cup heavy cream

2 tsp. licorice granules or licorice powder

Mini Raspberry Meringues

(1 tray)

1 oz. egg whites

3–4 drops lemon juice

2 tbsp. cane sugar

3½ tbsp. powdered sugar

1–1½ tbsp. raspberry purée (blended fresh or frozen and thawed raspberries)

2 chocolate cookies

⅓ cup fresh raspberries

optional: licorice granules to sprinkle on top

Cut up the white chocolate and put it in a bowl. Put the cream and licorice granules into a saucepan. Bring to a boil and whisk until the powder dissolves. Let it cool for a few minutes, then pour it into the bowl with the chocolate. Stir until the chocolate has melted. Cover the bowl with plastic wrap and put it in the refrigerator for at least 12 hours.

Take the bowl out of the refrigerator and beat the mixture into a fluffy mousse using an electric mixer. Divide the mousse into glasses for serving.

Preheat the oven to 210° F. Beat the egg whites and lemon juice for the meringue until foamy. Reduce the speed of the mixer and mix in half the sugar. Add the remaining sugar, then increase the speed of the mixer and beat for several minutes. Sift the powdered sugar into the meringue and fold it in with a rubber spatula. Next, gently mix in the raspberry purée.

Fill a disposable piping bag with the meringue and pipe small meringues onto a baking sheet lined with parchment paper. Bake in the middle of the oven for 15–20 minutes. Keep an eye on the meringues towards the end to make sure they do not turn brown and lose their pink color.

Crush the chocolate cookies and sprinkle the crumbs over the mousse. Place some meringues on top, then garnish with the raspberries and some licorice granules.

Strawberries with Licorice Sugar and Melted White Chocolate

■ If you haven't tried the combination of strawberries and licorice, try it now with this recipe. It's beautiful, fun, and tasty. And easy!

SERVINGS: 8–10

2 pints of strawberries
7 oz. white chocolate
2 tbsp. cane sugar
1 tbsp. licorice granules or crushed
  Turkish pepper

Put the strawberries in a bowl. Cut up the white chocolate and melt it on low power in the microwave. Stop the microwave occasionally and stir the chocolate to avoid burning it, or melt the chocolate in a water bath. Pour the chocolate into a bowl, preferably a chocolate fondue bowl with a burner underneath.

Combine the sugar and licorice and put the mixture into little bowls. Dip the strawberries in the melted white chocolate and then directly into the licorice sugar.

Milk Chocolate and Licorice Fondue
Cut up and melt 7 oz. of milk chocolate. Add ⅔ cup warm cream, 3 teaspoons of licorice granules, or 4 teaspoons licorice powder. If desired, add 1 tablespoon of whiskey. Pour into a bowl, preferably a chocolate fondue bowl with a burner underneath.

Serve with fruit and marshmallow skewers dipped in the melted chocolate. Another option is to serve with fresh strawberries and ice cream.

"PERFECT WITH CHILLED CHAMPAGNE OR SPARKLING WINE."

FOOD

Licorice Gratinéed Norway Lobster with Fennel Salad

■ This dish is ideal as a starter or light main dish. This salad is best when you use a kitchen mandoline to slice the vegetables.

SERVINGS: 10

Fennel Salad
½ of a fennel
1 lemon, finely grated zest and juice
1 tbsp. olive oil
1 yellow beet
1 chioggia beet
4 stalks of green asparagus
2 tbsp. fresh dill
sea salt
black pepper

Licorice Butter
3½ oz. butter, room temperature
1½ tsp. licorice granules
3 tbsp. freshly grated Parmesan cheese
1 tsp. chopped dill or fennel dill

20 Norway lobsters

Preheat the oven to 480° F. Trim and thinly slice the fennel for the salad. Drizzle some lemon juice and olive oil over the fennel slices. Thinly slice the beet and asparagus.

Layer the fennel, beet, and asparagus slices in a bowl. Sprinkle with dill, lemon zest, sea salt, and pepper.

Stir together the butter, licorice granules, Parmesan, and dill. Slice the lobsters open lengthwise and put them on a tray with the cut sides facing up. Spread the licorice butter on top and bake for 4–5 minutes.

Serve with the salad.

"A GLASS OF CHILLED CHAMPAGNE IS EXCELLENT WITH THIS LOBSTER DISH."

Scallops with Licorice Balsamic and Cauliflower Purée

■ A beautiful dish with wonderful flavors. Can be served as an appetizer or finger food.

SERVINGS: 4

Licorice Balsamic
¼ cup + 2 tbsp. red balsamic vinegar
1 tsp. honey
½ tsp. licorice granules or grated raw licorice stick

Cauliflower Purée
7 oz. cauliflower or Romanesco
¼ cup + 2 tbsp. vegetable stock
3 tbsp. whipping cream
¼ tsp. salt
⅛ tsp. white pepper

1 tbsp. butter
12 scallops
salt
black pepper

Garnish
fresh herbs, such as coriander, chervil, or dill
licorice granules or grated raw licorice stick

Boil the balsamic vinegar, honey, and licorice granules until the mixture reaches a syrup-like texture. Note that the liquid thickens a bit after cooling.

Trim and roughly chop the cauliflower. Save a few nice little bunches of cauliflower for garnish. Boil the cauliflower in the vegetable stock and cream until it gets soft, 5–10 minutes. Pour the stock mixture into a bowl and set aside. Blend the cauliflower into a smooth purée, adding enough of the stock mixture to reach the desired consistency. For a smoother purée, you can sift it through a sieve. Add the salt and pepper. Fill a disposable piping bag with the purée.

Melt the butter in a pan, then quickly fry the scallops on both sides. Add salt and pepper to taste.

Put the scallops on plates and pipe or spoon out the purée on the side. Drizzle the licorice balsamic over the top, then garnish with fresh herbs and little bunches of raw cauliflower. Finish by sprinkling with some licorice granules.

Shrimp with Licorice Aioli and Toasted Sourdough Bread

■ An aioli flavored with garlic, lime, and licorice is a true sensation for the palate with some nice shrimp. If the aioli feels too thick, just thin it out with some water.

SERVINGS: 4–6

Licorice Aioli

1 egg yolk
⅛ tbsp. salt
1 slice of garlic, finely chopped
2 tsp. freshly squeezed lime juice
lime zest, finely grated, optional
½ cup rapeseed or sunflower oil
½ tsp. ground licorice root
a pinch of black or cayenne pepper

6 large slices of sourdough bread
2 lbs. shrimp with shells
1 lemon, sliced
dill for garnish
1 pinch of black or cayenne pepper

To make the aioli, put the yolk in a bowl, then add the salt, garlic, and lime juice. If desired, add the lime zest. Add the oil in a thin stream while whisking until the mixture thickens. Next, add the ground licorice root while whisking, then add pepper to taste.

Toast or fry the sourdough bread with some butter and dish up on plates with the shrimp, aioli, and lemon slices. Garnish with dill and serve.

"I RECOMMEND THAT THE INGREDIENTS FOR THE AIOLI ARE AT ROOM TEMPERATURE."

Licorice Moules with French Fries

■ Classic moules-frites with a new twist! Namely, the mild taste of licorice root, pastis, and fennel. Before boiling the mussels, make sure they are alive by knocking lightly on the shells. If the mussels close, they are alive. Throw away those that do not close.

SERVINGS: 4–6

French Fries

6–8 potatoes
3–3½ cups neutral oil for deep-frying
salt

Licorice Moules

4½ lbs. fresh blue mussels
3 shallots
3–4 slices of garlic
½ fennel
1 oz. butter
2 tbsp. oil
2 licorice roots or ½–1 tsp. ground
*   licorice root*
2½ cups dry white wine
½ fl. oz. pastis (anise liqueur)
1¼ cups heavy cream
sea salt
white pepper
optional: 2 tbsp. chopped dill or fennel
*   dill*
1 lemon, finely grated zest

Clean the potatoes and slice them into ½-inch-thick sticks. Place them in cold water for 15–20 minutes. Drain the water and dry the potatoes with paper towels. Heat the oil to about 340° F in a large, deep saucepan or pot. Add the potatoes to the oil in batches and deep-fry until they're tender in the center and turn a nice color. It takes a few minutes. Let the fries drain on some paper towels and sprinkle them with salt.

Brush the mussels, removing the beard, and rinse them well. Peel and finely chop the shallots and garlic. Trim and finely chop the fennel.

Melt the butter in a big pot, add the oil, shallots, garlic, fennel, and licorice root and stir. Add the wine and pastis. Bring to a boil, then add the mussels and stir. Put on the lid and boil vigorously for 3–5 minutes. Remove the mussels from the pot and place them in a saucepan or bowl and cover to keep them warm (pick out and throw away any mussels that do not open).

Boil the broth in the pot until it is reduced by half. Add the cream and boil. Add salt and pepper to taste. Put the mussels back into the pot, stir once, then boil for approximately 30 seconds. Top with dill and lemon zest.

Lemon Aioli

This easily prepared lemon aioli goes well with the mussels: Combine ½ cup of mayonnaise, a finely chopped slice of garlic, 1 teaspoon of finely grated lemon zest, and 1 teaspoon of lemon juice. Add salt and pepper to taste.

Licorice Cured Baked Hake or Salmon with Raw Salad

■ For this recipe, I only cure the fish briefly since it is going into the oven. Serve the fish and salad with boiled potatoes and hard bread with aged cheese.

SERVINGS: 4

1 ¾ lbs. hake or salmon filet, peeled
1 tbsp. salt
1 tbsp. cane sugar
½ tsp. licorice granules or 1 tsp. ground licorice root
½ tsp. ground anise seeds
1 tbsp. fresh dill
butter for the pan

Raw Salad

½ fennel
1 chioggia beet
½ lemon, finely grated zest and juice
2 tbsp. olive or rapeseed oil
2 tbsp. fresh dill
sea salt
black pepper

Crème Fraîche Sauce with Dill

¾ cup crème fraîche
1 tsp. Dijon mustard
1 tsp. honey
1 tbsp. chopped dill
salt
white pepper

Garnish

black lumpfish roe
dill
blood lime or common lime

Put the fish on a plate. Combine the salt, sugar, licorice granules, and anise seeds, then strew the mixture over both sides of the fish. Sprinkle on some dill, then cover with plastic and place in the refrigerator for 1 hour. Meanwhile, preheat the oven to 250° F.

Put the fish, skin side up, in a greased baking dish and bake for 20–25 minutes.

Trim and thinly slice the fennel for the salad (preferably using a mandoline). Clean and slice the beet. Place the fennel and beet slices in layers in a bowl. Combine the lemon juice, zest, and olive oil, then pour over the salad. Add the dill, as well as the sea salt and black pepper, to taste.

Mix together the ingredients for the crème fraîche sauce.

Dish out the salad and fish on plates. Garnish with lumpfish roe, dill, and lime and serve with the dill sauce.

"THE BLOOD LIME LOOKS BEAUTIFUL WITH THE FISH, BUT COMMON LIME WORKS TOO, OF COURSE."

Fish Soup with Ground Licorice Root and Fennel Topping

■ A warm soup topped with a crispy salad. Different, and very tasty!

SERVINGS: 4

Fennel Topping

1 tsp. lemon oil
1 fennel
½ carrot
½ lemon, finely grated zest and juice

Fish Soup

1 onion
butter for frying
1⅔ pints fish stock
1¼ cups light or regular cream
1 tsp. ground licorice root or 2 whole licorice roots
½ lb. salmon filet, peeled
½ lb. haddock or hake filet, peeled
⅓ lb. shrimp with shells
salt
a few pinches of finely chopped, fresh chervil
black pepper

Pour the lemon oil into a bowl. Trim and thinly slice half of the fennel (preferably with a mandoline). Peel and thinly slice the carrot. Add the fennel and carrot slices to the oil. Add the lemon zest and a few drops of lemon juice and mix carefully. Set aside.

Dice the remaining half of the fennel. Peel and chop the onion. Melt some butter in a saucepan and fry the fennel and onion. Add the stock and let it boil for approximately 10 minutes, or until the vegetables have softened. Add the cream and the ground licorice root.

Dice the fish into 1-inch-wide pieces and steam them for 3–4 minutes or simmer for a couple of minutes in a saucepan with lightly salted water. Drain the water.

Dish out the fish and shrimp into bowls. If you used whole licorice roots, remove them from the soup. Blend the soup with a stick blender, then add salt to taste. Pour the soup into the bowls and sprinkle on some chervil and black pepper. Finish by garnishing the soup with the fennel topping.

Duck Breast with Licorice Glaze and Port Wine Boiled Figs

■ Fantastic flavors in this attractive dish.

SERVINGS: 4–6

Port Wine Boiled Figs

1 cup cane sugar
1 ¼ cups water
¾ cup port wine
6 fresh figs

Licorice Glaze

1 tsp. whiskey
1 tsp. licorice granules
2 tbsp. Japanese soy sauce
3 tbsp. sweet chili sauce
½ tbsp. honey
1 tbsp. olive oil

Duck Breasts

2 duck breasts with fat cap
salt and pepper
chervil or cicely for garnish

Jerusalem Artichoke Purée

14 oz. Jerusalem artichokes
½ shallot
¼ cup + 2 tbsp. heavy cream
salt and white pepper

Red Wine Gravy

¾ cup red wine
¾ cup dark meat stock
1 tsp. cornstarch
1–2 tsp. butter, room temperature
salt and black pepper

Preheat the oven to 300° F. Put the sugar, water, and port wine for the figs into a saucepan and simmer for a few minutes until it reaches a syrup consistency. Add the figs and continue simmering for 8–10 minutes, depending on the ripeness of the figs. Remove the figs from the pan and place them in a bowl. Boil the syrup for a few more minutes, then pour it over the figs.

Mix together the whiskey and licorice granules for the glaze. Stir until the granules have dissolved. Stir in the remaining ingredients for the glaze until fully combined.

Cut grooves into the fat caps of the duck breasts. Sear the duck breast in a dry frying pan with the fat caps facing down until they turn a nice color, then turn the breasts over and fry the other side. Add salt and pepper to taste. Put the duck breasts into a roasting pan and bake for 15–20 minutes, or until the centers of the breasts reach a temperature of 136–140° F. Wrap them in aluminum foil and let them rest for 10 minutes.

To make the purée, peel, chop, and boil the Jerusalem artichokes for 10–15 minutes, or until they soften. Peel, chop, and fry the shallots in oil until they soften. Drain the water from the artichokes and blend them with the shallots and cream. Add salt and pepper to taste.

Boil down the red wine and stock for the gravy by half. Thicken with cornstarch mixed with a splash of cold water. Whisk in the butter or use a stick blender. Add salt and pepper to taste.

Brush the duck breasts with the glaze then slice them. Garnish with chervil or cicely and serve immediately with figs, purée, sauce, and any remaining glaze.

Wild Stew with Licorice Root and Black Trumpet Mushrooms

■ Game meat is not a requirement for this rich stew—beef or lamb works just as well. Serve with boiled potatoes and black currant jelly.

SERVINGS: 4

butter for frying
1⅓ lbs. game meat, such as moose or deer, cut into pieces
¾ cup red wine
2 pints dark meat stock
2 licorice roots
⅔ tsp. anise seeds
2 bay leaves
⅛ tsp. crushed or ground black pepper
6 small onions or 1 yellow onion
3 purple or regular carrots
2 parsnips
5 oz. black trumpet or chanterelle mushrooms
¾ cup heavy cream
1 tbsp. flour
a few sprigs of fresh thyme

Melt the butter in a frying pan then sear the meat. Once seared, put the meat into a large pot. Add the wine and stock. Break the licorice roots in half and put them in the stew. Grind the anise seeds in a mortar, then add them to the stew with the bay leaves and black pepper. Bring the stew to a boil; once it has boiled a few minutes, skim if necessary. Reduce the heat, cover, and allow the stew to simmer for 50 minutes.

While the stew simmers, peel the onions, carrots and parsnips. Slice the onions and cut the root vegetables into small pieces. Add the vegetables to the stew and let it simmer another 40 minutes.

Meanwhile, trim the mushrooms and simmer them in lightly salted water for 3–4 minutes. Let them drain on some paper towels, then fry them in some butter.

Stir the cream into the stew and thicken with the flour mixed with a splash of cold water. Carefully mix the mushrooms into the stew and finish with a sprinkling of fresh thyme on top.

Licorice Marinated Lamb with Red Wine Gravy and Baked Sweet Potato

■ Lamb and licorice go surprisingly well together.

SERVINGS: 4

Marinade

1 tsp. licorice granules
1 tbsp. water
1 tbsp. Chinese soy sauce
1 tbsp. balsamic vinegar
¼ cup + 2 tbsp. olive oil
1 sprig of rosemary, roughly chopped
1–2 slices of garlic, roughly chopped

1⅓ lbs. lamb chops

Baked Sweet Potatoes

2 sweet potatoes
4 Purple Congo potatoes
2 tbsp. olive oil
1 whole garlic, with peel
6 small onions
6 sprigs of fresh thyme
salt

Red Wine or Madeira Gravy

1 shallot
½ carrot
1 tbsp. butter for frying
1 cup red wine or Madeira
½ cup dark meat stock
½–1 tbsp. balsamic vinegar
½–1 tbsp. honey
¼ tsp. cornstarch
1 tsp. butter, room temperature

salt and black pepper
1 cup Greek yogurt

Mix the licorice granules and water for the marinade together in a bowl. Stir until the granules have dissolved. Add the soy sauce, balsamic vinegar, and olive oil. Mix to combine, then add the rosemary and garlic. Put the lamb chops into a heavy plastic bag, then pour in the marinade. Close the bag and ensure that the marinade covers all of the meat. Place in the refrigerator for approximately 30 minutes.

Preheat the oven to 440° F. Wash, dry, and slice the potatoes. Put the slices on a baking sheet lined with parchment paper, then drizzle on the olive oil. Turn the potatoes over to ensure all the slices are oiled. Cut the garlic in half. Peel and cut the onions in half. Place them on the baking sheet with the potatoes and add the thyme. Bake for 20 minutes, or until the potatoes soften. Remove the pan from the oven then sprinkle with salt.

Peel and dice the shallot and carrot. Melt the butter in a saucepan, then fry the diced shallot and carrot for a few minutes. Add the red wine, meat stock, balsamic vinegar, and honey. Boil until half the liquid remains. Strain and thicken the gravy with cornstarch mixed with a splash of cold water. Whisk in the butter or use a stick blender to combine.

Remove the lamb chops from the refrigerator and pour out the marinade. Grill or sear the meat in butter for a few minutes on each side. Add salt and pepper to taste. Serve the lamb chops with the red wine gravy, potatoes, onions, and yogurt.

Barbecue Condiments

Licorice Salt
A nice alternative to ordinary salt for steak, entrecote, or game meat.

MAKES: ⅓ **CUP**

4 tbsp. sea salt
1 tsp. licorice granules
½ tbsp. dried, finely chopped garlic
½ tbsp. dried thyme
½ tbsp. chili flakes

Mix all the ingredients together, then store the salt in an airtight jar.

Barbecue Sauce Seasoned with Licorice
The licorice is only supposed to provide the slightest touch of flavor to this sauce. Too much will make it bitter. The sauce goes well with beef, pork, and chicken.

SERVINGS: 8

4–5 plum tomatoes
3 tbsp. cane sugar
3 tbsp. golden syrup
2 tbsp. red wine vinegar
⅓ cup water
2 tbsp. Worcestershire sauce
2 tbsp. Chinese soy sauce
½ tsp. licorice granules or 1 tsp. licorice powder

Dice the tomatoes then combine them with the rest of the ingredients in a stainless steel saucepan. Bring to a boil, then reduce the heat and simmer for 10 minutes while stirring. Blend the mixture with a stick blender and strain if necessary. Allow the sauce to cool before serving.

Licorice and Honey Glaze
This glaze is best paired with duck breasts or dark meat, such as steak, entrecôte, lamb, and game meat. Just brush it onto the meat after it is has been grilled. Heavenly!

MAKES: ½ **CUP**

1 tsp. whiskey
1 tsp. licorice granules
2 tbsp. Japanese soy sauce
3 tbsp. sweet chili sauce
3 tbsp. honey
1 tbsp. olive oil

Mix together the whiskey and licorice granules in a bowl. Stir until the granules have dissolved. Add the remaining ingredients and stir into a sauce.

Fresh Licorice Pasta, Minced Lamb Balls, and Yellow Tomato Sauce

■ Delicious homemade licorice pasta.

SERVINGS: 4–6

Fresh Licorice Pappardelle
2 cups durum flour
4 eggs
1 tbsp. ground licorice root
1 tbsp. licorice granules

Minced Lamb Balls
3 tbsp. breadcrumbs
3 tbsp. milk
3 tbsp. heavy cream
1 lb. minced lamb
2 tbsp. chopped fresh rosemary
1 tbsp. chopped fresh coriander
2 finely chopped garlic slices
2 tbsp. chopped yellow onion
1 egg
1 tsp. salt
¼ tsp. ground black pepper
butter and olive oil for frying

Yellow Tomato Sauce
1 yellow onion
1 container yellow cherry tomatoes
2 vine tomatoes
½ red pepper
2 tbsp. cold-pressed olive oil
2 slices of garlic
1–2 tbsp. honey
1 tbsp. balsamic vinegar
½ tsp. salt
¼ tsp. ground white pepper
*1½ oz. grated Parmesan or aged Svecia
  cheese*

Pour the flour into a pile on a work space and make a hole in the center. Crack open the eggs into the hole and work them into the flour with a fork, a little at the time. Add the licorice once the dough is grainy and then knead into a smooth, semi-solid dough. Put the dough in a plastic bag and place in the refrigerator for 30 minutes.

Divide the dough into four pieces and roll it out thinly with a pasta maker or by hand. Slice the dough into strips, about ½ inch wide and 10 inches long. Hang the pasta and let it dry at room temperature for 2–5 hours.

Pour the breadcrumbs for the meatballs into a large bowl. Add the milk and cream. Stir until combined, then let the mixture rest for a couple of minutes. Add the remaining ingredients and stir into a smooth mixture. Roll the mixture into balls, then fry them in butter and olive oil until they are cooked through. If desired, add a little more salt and pepper.

Peel and finely chop the onion for the tomato sauce. Dice the tomatoes and pepper. Fry the onions, tomatoes, and pepper with the oil in a saucepan. Finely chop the garlic and stir into the mixture along with the honey and vinegar. Add the salt and pepper and let the sauce simmer for 8–10 minutes.

Boil the pasta al dente, 3–4 minutes. Serve it with the meatballs and tomato sauce. Top with some grated cheese.

Cheeses with Licorice Glazed Apricots and Licorice Toasted Almonds

■ These delicious condiments for the cheese plate can be done in a jiffy! I recommend dessert cheeses like blue cheese, soft cheese, and brie.

SERVINGS: 6–8

Licorice Caramelized Almonds

3½ oz. almonds
½ tsp. oil
1 tbsp. cane sugar
½ tsp. licorice granules
½ tsp. salt

Licorice Glazed Apricots

8 fresh apricots
2 tbsp. honey
1 tsp. licorice granules or licorice powder

Pour the almonds and oil into a warm saucepan and toast for a few minutes while stirring. Sprinkle on the sugar and let it melt, then sprinkle on the licorice granules and salt. Toss quickly, then put the almonds on a piece of parchment paper and let them cool.

Cut the apricots in half and core them. Place them in a frying pan and drizzle with the honey. Fry on low heat until the apricots turn golden. Sprinkle with the licorice granules, then put the apricots in a bowl and serve them warm with the cheese.

"THE JAM ON THE NEXT PAGE ALSO GOES WELL WITH THESE CHEESES."

Licorice Hard Bread with Cheese and Cherry and Licorice Jam

■ A blue cheese is the best imaginable complement to the hard bread and cherry jam duo. I use granulated sugar for the jam since the cherries do not contain enough of the gelatin substance pectin.

Cherry and Licorice Jam
Use an olive corer if available—an excellent tool for saving time when coring olives or cherries.

MAKES: 2 JARS
2 pints fresh cherries
2 tbsp. water
½ tbsp. licorice granules
2 cups granulated sugar

Licorice Hard Bread
Easy to bake and to eat!

MAKES: 8 PIECES
1 cup low-fat milk
1 tbsp. honey
1 tbsp. sunflower or rapeseed oil
⅓ oz. yeast
½ tsp. salt
1 tsp. licorice granules
1 tsp. ground licorice root
¾ cup coarse rye flour
1⅓ cups flour

Core the cherries and put them in a saucepan with the water and licorice granules. Stir and bring to a boil, then reduce heat and let simmer approximately 10 minutes. Stir in the sugar and simmer another 4–5 minutes. Skim off if needed and pour into hot sterilized jars. Put on the lids, then let cool. Store them in a cool location.

Stir together the milk, honey, oil, yeast, salt, licorice granules, and licorice root in a bowl. Stir in the rye flour, then add the remaining flour, a little at a time. Work into a smooth dough. Put the dough in a plastic bag and place it in the refrigerator for 30 minutes. Meanwhile, preheat the oven to 440° F.

Divide the dough into eight equal pieces, powder with some rye flour, then roll out the dough into flat, thin, round pieces. Place them on a lightly floured or parchment paper-lined baking sheet. Prick the dough with a fork. Bake for 5–7 minutes or until the edges darken. Let the bread cool on a rack.

DRINKS

Licorice Schnapps

Licorice and Rosemary

I made this schnapps for the first time a few years ago on a television show at midsummer's eve. It is one of my absolute favorites. The licorice and rosemary give it a well-balanced and homogenous flavor. Served chilled, it's hard to beat.

MAKES: 1½ PINTS

2 licorice roots
2 twigs of fresh rosemary
1½ pints unseasoned vodka
1 bottle, 1½ pint
2–3 tsp. cane or raw sugar, optional

Put the licorice roots, rosemary, and vodka into the bottle and let it sit for five to six days. Strain, then add the sugar if desired. Shake the bottle to incorporate the sugar.

Licorice and Melon

This is really good and can also be used for mixed drinks.

MAKES: 1½ PINTS

2 licorice roots
3½ oz. melon, cut into small pieces (preferably galia or cantaloupe with orange pulp)
1½ pints unseasoned vodka
1 bottle, 1½ pint

Put the licorice roots, melon, and vodka in the bottle and let it sit for five to six days. Strain. Serve chilled.

Licorice and Lemon

A refreshing schnapps, this can also be used for mixed drinks. Just wash the lemon thoroughly and peel the outer zest with a knife.

MAKES: 1½ PINTS

2 licorice roots
1 lemon, zested
1½ pints unseasoned vodka
1 bottle, 1½ pint
2–3 tsp. cane or raw sugar, optional

Put the licorice roots, lemon zest, and vodka in the bottle and let it sit for five to six days. Strain. Add the sugar if desired, then shake the bottle to incorporate the sugar. Serve chilled.

Licorice, Sweet Gale, and St. John's Wort

A sophisticated licorice schnapps with a nice touch of sweet gale and St. John's wort.

MAKES: 1½ PINTS

2 licorice roots
dried leaves from 2 sprigs of sweet gale
1/15 oz. dried St. John's wort
1½ pints unseasoned vodka
2–3 tsp. cane or raw sugar, optional

Put the licorice roots and herbs into the vodka and let it sit for 5–6 days. Strain through a coffee filter, add sugar if desired, and shake the bottle. Serve chilled.

Licorice Liqueurs, Cocktails, and Shots

Licorice Root Liqueur

■ Tasty and mild licorice liqueur. Delicious with desserts or with a cup of coffee.

MAKES: 1 PINT

3 licorice roots
¾ pint unseasoned vodka
⅕ pint Irish whiskey or bourbon, non-smoky
⅓ cup raw sugar
1 tbsp. honey

Put the licorice roots into the bottle and add the vodka. Let it sit in the refrigerator for 1 month. Strain, then add the sugar and honey. Cover the bottle and shake until the honey and sugar dissolve.

Licorice Cocktail

■ For an added touch, rub the edge of the glass with a lime and then dip it into some licorice sugar (see the recipe on page 96).

SERVINGS: 1

1 glass of ice
1 fl. oz. licorice root liqueur or licorice liqueur
ginger ale
1 slice of lime

Shake the ice and licorice liqueur. Pour into a chilled cocktail glass then fill with ginger ale. Garnish with a slice of lime.

Black Licorice Liqueur

■ This liqueur has a stronger licorice taste than the cocktail made with licorice roots. (See the picture on page 127.)

MAKES: 1 PINT

⅗ pint unseasoned vodka
2 tbsp. licorice granules or raw licorice pastilles
⅓ cup raw sugar

Combine the vodka and licorice in a bottle and shake. Let it sit overnight. If using licorice pastilles, let it sit for 1–2 days, until the pastilles have melted. Add the sugar and shake until the sugar dissolves.

Warm Licorice Shot with Coffee

Fill a shot glass one-third with licorice root liqueur or black licorice liqueur. Add an equal amount of hot coffee, then top with whipped cream and licorice powder or granules.

Licorice Shot with Peppermint

Add a few drops of peppermint oil to the bottle of licorice root liqueur or black licorice liqueur. Done!

WINE AND OTHER BEVERAGES

Licorice can be challenging to find drinks for, but also exciting.

■ **For sweet licorice**, such as premium licorice or licorice boats, prosecco, an Italian sparkling wine, works well. For example, Pizzolato or a sweet Asti. Both of them also go well with licorice ice cream, ice cream cake, rhubarb cake with licorice meringues, and licorice macarons.

■ **For salty licorice**, a tart and refreshing sauvignon blanc from Australia or Champagne can be a thrill. The Portuguese dessert wine Moscatel de Setúbal or a sweet and refreshing Late Harvest Orange Muscat and Flora works as well. Another completely different drink to try is Angostura bitters.

■ **For raw licorice**, I suggest champagne or a pinot noir from Australia.

■ **For licorice toffee**, chocolate-dipped licorice butterscotch, and licorice chocolate, I suggest a sweet Malbec from Argentina, such as Malamado, whose flavor reminds me of port wine and is made the same way. A shiraz, like Tabalí shiraz, or a syrah are two other alternatives. A white wine, like Kloster Eberbach Riesling Kabinett, will be a completely different experience.

■ **For fish and seafood seasoned with licorice**, I recommend chardonnay aged in oak, with a touch of butter, for example, Penfold's Thomas Hyland from Australia, or champagne.

■ **For licorice-seasoned meat dishes**, licorice and chocolate cakes with strong flavors, or desserts with a distinct touch of licorice, I recommend red wines such as amarone from Italy, for example Masi, or a masculine pinotage from South Africa, like Diemersfontein.

■ **Beer with licorice:** A dark, creamy glass of Guinness, stout, or draught is the best choice. The next choice is, quite unexpectedly, light wheat beer. There are also many good beers flavored with real licorice, like Johan Bülow's licorice stout and Amarelli's dark or light licorice beers.

■ **Liquor and licorice:** The combinations of whiskey or dark rum with ice and licorice, or licorice and chocolate, are my favorites. Especially with Jack Daniel's Tennessee Honey. Grappa or Sambuca are two other drinks that go well with licorice. And please try a chilled Limoncello Biostilla served with a licorice dessert.

LICORICE TASTING

Organizing a licorice tasting is both easy and fun. And the tasting itself is also a very enjoyable experience!

I usually put different kinds of licorice on a small plate, starting with raw products and refined raw products, about half a teaspoon of each. Then I lay out flavor combinations, for example, a piece of licorice candy with chili or salmiak, a piece of licorice and chocolate butterscotch or some licorice chocolate. Then I finish with something baked, like macarons. Serve water or sparkling water while tasting.

Arrange the different samples on a plate:

■ A piece of licorice root.

■ Some whole anise and fennel seeds. This is to illustrate the difference between real licorice and these herbs, which naturally taste like licorice. (For more information, see page 8.)

■ Ground licorice root.

■ Spray-dried licorice powder.

■ Salty licorice powder containing salmiak.

■ Licorice granules or raw licorice pastilles.

Begin with these raw products and their refined versions. Then move on to some other delicious treats:

■ A piece of soft licorice candy, for example, red licorice or some other exciting variant. Alternatively, licorice flavored with chili or salmiak.

■ A piece of licorice chocolate or chocolate-dipped licorice butterscotch, just to introduce the fantastic combination of licorice and chocolate.

■ A licorice macaron (see the recipe on page 64) placed in the middle of the plate makes a nice finish. As a silver lining, serve a glass of chilled champagne or prosecco with the macaron.

Tip!
You can cleanse the palate between each sample with a piece of lemon, a fresh raspberry, or a mint leaf.

THE HISTORY OF LICORICE CANDY

The development of licorice candy started in seventeenth-century England, when a man named George Saville started producing medicinal licorice pills that were stamped by hand in order to look like money. The pills were called Pontefract cakes, or sometimes Yorkshire pennies, and they are still produced today.

Another George, George Dunhill, was a pharmacist in a licorice-growing family in England. In 1760, he brewed a mixture of licorice extract, treacle, sugar, and flour, which became the basis for the English licorice confectionery. That marked licorice's transformation from medicine to candy!

In Sweden, pharmacies started selling licorice roots in the nineteenth century, and at the end of the century they started making licorice candies in molds.

In the early twentieth century, the first boxes of Läkerol were produced in Gävle, Sweden. The name has its origin in "läker allt" (cures all), and was at first the name of an antiseptic liquid. But after making an inspirational trip to Germany, where he tasted cough drops of mint, licorice, and gum arabic, wholesaler Adolf Ahlgren decided to make a pill instead of a liquid medicine. He used gum arabic, a resin from the African Acacia tree and a natural substance that is still used today when making soft and chewy licorice candy.

Until a few years ago, not much was happening on the licorice front. We had Lakrisal and some other forms of sweet and salty licorice, but today, thankfully, things are a lot different. New licorice candies are announced at an amazing rate—both completely new candy variants and classic candies flavored with licorice. On top of that, there is a lot of quality licorice products and even some organic licorice candies. In other words, there is a lot of licorice for you to enjoy.

Warning!

Excessive consumption of licorice can cause high blood pressure, headaches, nausea, diarrhea, edema (abnormal fluid retention), sodium imbalance, and hypokalemia (low potassium levels).

Pregnant women, diabetics, and anyone with high blood pressure should consume with caution, as should persons with serious liver and kidney diseases or potassium deficiency.

LICORICE FESTIVALS

Around the World and Licorice Day in the USA

■ **Stockholm Licorice Festival**
The first licorice festival in Stockholm was held in 2009. Since then, the number of visitors has increased each year, with 11,0000 people attending the April event in 2015.
www.lakritsfestivalen.se

■ **Gothenburg Chocolate, Licorice, and Delicacy Festival**
This festival takes place in the heart of Gothenburg. It serves as a meeting place for all licorice lovers, licorice producers, and retailers.
www.chokladkalaset.se

■ **Copenhagen Licorice Festival**
Denmark also has their own festival, Lakridsfestivalen, a journey through the flavor of licorice, in Copenhagen.
www.lakridsfestival.dk

■ **Helsinki Salmiakki Gala**
An annual event in February. Here the salmiak product of the year is awarded the Salmiakki Finlandia.
www.salmiakki.fi

■ **Pontefract Liquorice Festival, England**
Pontefract is a town in Yorkshire, England, which hosts an annual licorice festival in mid-July. The town has a long history of licorice, since licorice has been grown there since the sixteenth century. Although almost all harvesting ceased in the mid-1900s due to low profits and competition from imported licorice.
www.pontefractliquoricefestival.co.uk

■ **Oklahoma Licorice Festival, USA**
Each year in April a licorice festival is held at Aunt Gertrude's House, Guthrie, Oklahoma. Here you can find a wide range of licorice products from all around the world—Australia, England, Finland, Holland, New Zealand, Sweden, and, of course, the USA. You can also find Virgil's Root Beer with licorice!
www.auntgertrudeshouse.com

■ **Licorice Day in the USA**
National Licorice Day is held on April 12 each year. This celebration of licorice is starting to spread to the Nordic region, too. In the USA and Australia, red licorice is quite common. It's a sweeter licorice candy complemented with berry flavors.

Where to Buy

Licorice granules, licorice powder, salty licorice powder, licorice syrup and ground licorice root:
www.queenoflicorice.se
www.mediamat.se
www.lakritsroten.se

Licorice pasta and aroma, black powder coloring, liquid black food coloring, and salmiak salt:
www.essencefabriken.se

Pictured, from left to right: licorice roots, raw licorice, and gum arabic.

CONVERSION CHARTS

METRIC AND IMPERIAL CONVERSIONS

(These conversions are rounded for convenience)

Ingredient	Cups/Tablespoons/ Teaspoons	Ounces	Grams/Milliliters
Baking powder	1 teaspoon	0.125 ounce	3.5 grams
Berries, fresh	1 cup	4.5–5 ounces	125–140 grams
Cocoa powder	1 tablespoon	0.2 ounce	5 grams
Coconut, grated	1 tablespoon	0.15 ounce	4.7 grams
Flour, all-purpose	1 cup/1 tablespoon	4.5 ounces/0.3 ounces	125 grams/8 grams
Fruit, dried	1 cup	4 ounces	120 grams
Fruits or veggies, chopped	1 cup	5 to 7 ounces	145 to 200 grams
Fruits or veggies, puréed	1 cup	8.5 ounces	245 grams
Honey or maple syrup	1 tablespoon	.75 ounces	20 grams
Liquids: milk or cream	1 cup	8 fluid ounces	240 milliliters
Oats	1 cup	5.5 ounces	150 grams
Quinoa, uncooked	1 cup	6 ounces	170 grams
Salt	1 teaspoon	0.2 ounces	6 grams
Sugar, cane	1 cup	8 ounces	200 grams
Sugar, powdered	1 cup	4 ounces	28 grams
Yeast	3 tablespoons	1 ounce	28 grams

OVEN TEMPERATURES

Fahrenheit	Celsius	Gas Mark
225°	110°	¼
250°	120°	½
275°	140°	1
300°	150°	2
325°	160°	3
350°	180°	4
375°	190°	5
400°	200°	6
425°	220°	7
450°	230°	8

Index

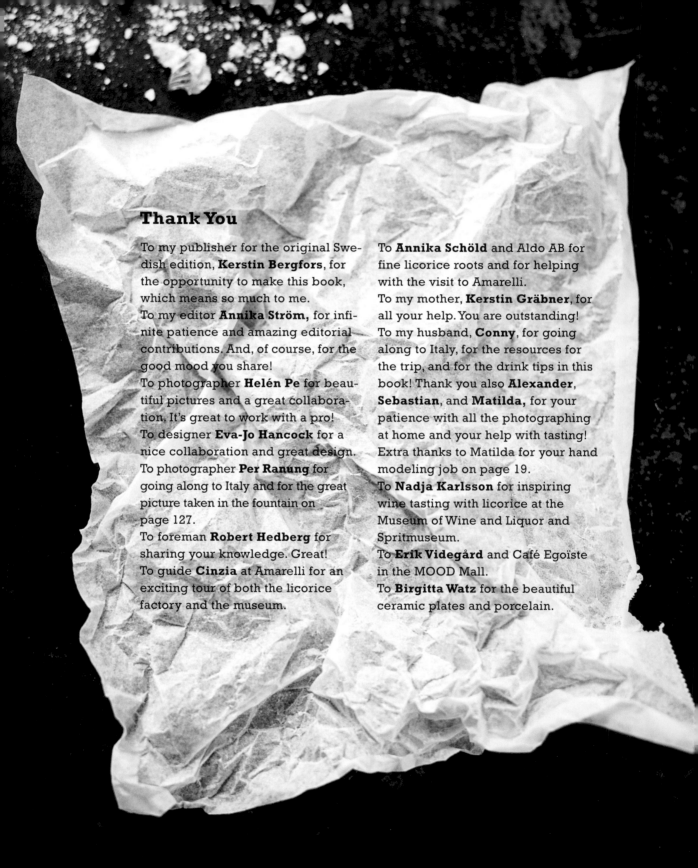

Thank You

To my publisher for the original Swedish edition, **Kerstin Bergfors**, for the opportunity to make this book, which means so much to me.

To my editor **Annika Ström,** for infinite patience and amazing editorial contributions. And, of course, for the good mood you share!

To photographer **Helén Pe** for beautiful pictures and a great collaboration. It's great to work with a pro!

To designer **Eva-Jo Hancock** for a nice collaboration and great design.

To photographer **Per Ranung** for going along to Italy and for the great picture taken in the fountain on page 127.

To foreman **Robert Hedberg** for sharing your knowledge. Great!

To guide **Cinzia** at Amarelli for an exciting tour of both the licorice factory and the museum.

To **Annika Schöld** and Aldo AB for fine licorice roots and for helping with the visit to Amarelli.

To my mother, **Kerstin Gräbner**, for all your help. You are outstanding!

To my husband, **Conny**, for going along to Italy, for the resources for the trip, and for the drink tips in this book! Thank you also **Alexander**, **Sebastian**, and **Matilda,** for your patience with all the photographing at home and your help with tasting! Extra thanks to Matilda for your hand modeling job on page 19.

To **Nadja Karlsson** for inspiring wine tasting with licorice at the Museum of Wine and Liquor and Spritmuseum.

To **Erik Videgård** and Café Egoïste in the MOOD Mall.

To **Birgitta Watz** for the beautiful ceramic plates and porcelain.